ANGELS SPEAK

THE FOUNDATION STONE MEDITATION

Rudolf Steiner

ANGELS SPEAK
THE FOUNDATION STONE MEDITATION

contemplations

Selected and Introduced by

Michiel ter Horst

SteinerBooks
2025

2025
SteinerBooks
an imprint of Anthropsophic Press, Inc.
834 Main Street, PO Box 358
Spencertown, New York 12165
www.steinerbooks.org

 This book is a translation of *Engelen spreken de Grondsteenspreuk*, originally published in Dutch by SteinerVertalingen (2023).

Translation by
Philip Mees

ISBN: 978-1-62148-388-5
eBook ISBN: 978-1-62148-389-2

Printed in the United States of America
by Integrated Books International

CONTENTS

PREFACE

A YEAR AFTER THE FIRE of the first Goetheanum Rudolf Steiner stood full of energy in the over-full carpentry shop behind the burned ruins. For eight days, from Christmas Day 1923 through New Year's Day 1924 he laid, as he called it, together with the 800 people present, the Foundation Stone "in our hearts" as a meditation. Every day at 10 in the morning, and on the last day also in the evening—nine times in total—he spoke the verses, not always exactly the same, but with certain differences. In doing so he evoked the angelic hierarchies with the question to let their voices sound for us in the spirit. In this meditation each hierarchy responds with a meditative content that originates from early Christianity, and was handed down in Latin in the tradition of the Rosicrucians. The Foundation Stone is therefore a purely spiritual text, not intended as information, but as meditation. In the course of that week, Rudolf Steiner chose for each day of the week a certain text that could be helpful in the meditative use of the verses.

Together with the consideration and establishment of the statutes and a series of evening lectures, this "Foundation Stone" formed the foundation of the General Anthroposophical Society as a worldwide organization. Its objective was to create a flexible unity in the patchwork of national and regional anthroposophical groups. After the Christmas Conference Rudolf Steiner wrote a public version of the Foundation Stone Meditation that was printed in the *Nachrichtenblatt* of January 13, 1924. In this public version he combined the Hebrew and Greek names of the angelic hierarchies, which he had evoked during the foundation meetings, as "Spirits of Strength", "Spirits of Light", and "Spirits of Soul."

However, in order to approach Rudolf Steiner's choice of words as closely as possible, and to do justice to the freshness and speed of his words, I have chosen to adapt, at some points, a frequently used and beautiful English translation of the printed version to the words as they sounded orally, with the Greek and Hebrew names of the angels and the Latin texts of the Rosicrucian sayings. As Rudolf Steiner formulated each panel of the text in five sentences, I accentuated those with a blank line each. The other variations on the widely used translation of the printed version are clarified in the chapter *Text and Translation* at the end of this book. The fivefold structure of each panel of the Foundation Stone Meditation, being fundamental to its structure, forms the layout of the text collection.

The Foundation Stone Meditation can be viewed as a seed form. The all-encompassing relationships of the cosmic ordering of the spiritual world, which Rudolf Steiner has sketched in his works and lectures, are bound together here in seed form. But that is not all. It was also the germ for the equally all-encompassing mystery of the Esoteric School he had announced in the Christmas meeting and anchored in the Statutes, and which he indeed started six weeks later. The evocation of the angelic hierarchies, which is present in the Foundation Stone in germinal form, would grow to cosmic dimensions in the Esoteric School. We may assume that Rudolf Steiner, when he laid the Foundation Stone in the hearts of those present, was able to oversee all the foregoing and everything he had resolved to do as a great panorama.

In this book some sixty meditative passages have been brought together from Rudolf Steiner's works about the role of the angels in cosmic and human development, to let the words of the

Foundation Stone Meditation appear in a new light. After this foreword the book begins with an English translation of the Meditation followed by an introduction to the cohesion of the text as a whole. Then follows the collection of contemplations relating to parts of the Meditation. At the end one will find clarifying notes and an explanation of the abbreviations.

This book is not easy reading, but contains matter to contemplate and most of all to let Rudolf Steiner's words speak while perhaps hearing the voices of angels whispering in our ears.

The Foundation Stone Meditation

Human soul
you live within the limbs
which bear you through the world of space
into the spirits' ocean-being.

Practice spirit-recalling
in depths of soul
where in the wielding
World-Creator-Being
your own I
comes into being
in the I of God
and you will truly live
in human world-all being.

For the Father-Spirit of the heights holds sway
in depths of worlds begetting life.

Seraphim – Cherubim – Thrones
let ring forth from the heights
what in the depths is echoed
speaking
Ex Deo nascimur.

This is heard by the spirits of the elements
in east, west, north, south
may human beings hear it.

Human soul
you live within the beat of heart and lung
which leads you through the rhythms of time
into the feeling of your own soul-being.

Practice spirit-sensing
in balance of the soul
where the surging
deeds of world-evolving
unite
your own I
with the I of the world
and you will truly feel
in human soul's creating.

For the Christ-will encircling us holds sway
in world rhythms, bestowing grace upon souls.

Kyriotetes – Dynameis – Exousiai
let from the east be enkindled
what through the west takes on form
and speaks
In Christo morimur.

This is heard by the spirits of the elements
in east, west, north, south
may human beings hear it.

Human soul
you live within the resting head
which from the grounds of eternity
unlocks for you world-thoughts.

Practice spirit-beholding
in stillness of thought
where the gods' eternal aims
bestow
the light of cosmic being
on your own I
for free and active willing
and you will truly think
in human spirit depths.

For the Spirit's world-thoughts hold sway
in cosmic being, imploring light.

Archai – Archangeloi – Angeloi
O let from the depths be entreated
what in the heights is heard
then it speaks through the world
Per Spiritum Sanctum reviviscimus.

This is heard by the spirits of the elements
in east, west, north, south
may human beings hear it.

At the turning point of time
the spirit-light of the world
entered the stream of earth existence.

Darkness of night
had ceased its reign.

Day-radiant light
shone forth in human souls
light
that gives warmth
to simple shepherds' hearts
light
that enlightens
the wise heads of kings.

Light divine
Christ-Sun
warm our hearts
enlighten our heads
that good may become
what from our hearts
we are founding
what from our heads
we direct
with focused will.

INTRODUCTION

Human soul!

An awe-inspiring call, this opening of the Foundation Stone Meditation! At the same time, it sounds very intimate. Every time again it calls forth new wonder, amazement, questions. What is the soul? What is the human soul? Am I, or do I have a soul? Human soul! Who is sounding this call, three times even? For my part, it prompts me to keep looking for insight into the soul, to look for *knowledge of higher worlds*. I reach for Rudolf Steiner's book *How to Know Higher Worlds*. The very first sentence is already about the human soul: "The capacities by which we can gain insights into higher worlds lie dormant within each one of us." Dormant capacities in each human soul? Can I awaken those? Some pages later we read that this requires a particular mood: "We begin with a fundamental mood of soul." A fundamental mood of soul. Rudolf Steiner calls this mood of soul *the path of veneration, of devotion.*

According to Socrates we can discover the world through wonder, astonishment, curiosity. Those three I am familiar with. But now we are asked to deepen these and strengthen them to *respect and admiration* if we really want to achieve insight into the human soul. A little later even this proves to be insufficient. For to gain insight into truth, into spirit, we are asked to intensify our mood again, now to *veneration and devotion to the truth.*

But in our time of the internet and social media veneration and devotion are not a matter of course. Criticism and making things look suspicious often triumph, and cultivation of a devoted mood is a rarity. You have to really use your will for it. Add to this that there is a lot of talk in the media without any real understanding of what is being said.

Interestingly, this phenomenon was brought home to me in commentaries on a new internet application in the sphere of artificial intelligence. The app is able to generate remarkably clear and informative texts. Only, those texts consist of learnt thoughts. The data are "pre-trained," which means that the app is not able to understand the text it has itself generated. Someone had entered a trick-question: "I have a problem when playing the piano, because I am getting a pain in the fingers of my right hand. Can you advise me?" The answer of the program was: "Look at your left hand. You'd expect to see fingers there too. Can't you use those?" That sounds stupid, but it is totally logical. The information is correct, but is neither useful nor meaningful. The program produces a text but does not understand it. It can write words like "astonishment, wonder, and reverence," but doesn't understand them, doesn't feel them. But let's be honest, how often does it happen that we do the same? I know I have myself talked a lot of blah-blah, not only in casual conversation, but also in serious discussions. Also in business situations. Who hasn't? But on the path of devotion you begin to change that.

Right at the beginning of the series of quoted passages, I put the above-mentioned fragment about the *path of veneration* for a very special reason. The *path of veneration* is at this time more important than ever, especially for anthroposophists. Why? Because of the *esoteric cycle* consisting of nineteen lessons of the School of Spiritual Science. Until 1992, these esoteric lessons were not officially available. They were imparted "from mouth to ear." At the time, Rudolf Steiner strongly insisted on keeping the texts secret, in order to carefully protect the sphere of veneration and devotion around these texts.

Following then-current practice, I also kept the texts strictly to myself, never talked about them, let alone participated in theoretical discussions about them. It is all too easy to twist the living thinking power of the words into dead concepts. But in the meantime these texts have lived in anthroposophical meditations for a century. They have taken on the power of form. The secrecy has been lifted; in 1992 they were published in German with the official consent of the leaders of the School of Spiritual Science. Since then they have become available on the internet and in many translations. In 2017 appeared for the first time a published English translation of the nineteen lessons and mantras. But now we have to be extra alert. Now we, without exhortations from Rudolf Steiner, have to produce the will power never to leave the path of veneration as we read the text. Guard these words with your clear thinking, care for them with your loving devotion, wake them to life with will power and concentration; otherwise these esoteric class lessons cannot reveal their content to you.

People who are deeply familiar with these texts may of course feel that the translation could be improved. There is nothing wrong with that, as long as it results in a deepening of your insight. But watch out for the voices of the two seductive Sirens along your way: on the right you hear soft whispering Know-It-All, on the left Letter Slave. Of course, I have also wrestled with those two sirens while translating, but I have also become friends with them. Eventually I noticed that, as I developed more insight in the meaning, the poetic beauty of the Foundation Stone Meditation spoke to me more and more, and the aspect of beauty of the Meditation became more and more important for me. Finally, I began to notice that the will power you have to generate to gain insight into this polished crystal with its twelvefold cohesion (more about this later) is perhaps its most important aspect. This leads you on the way to the world of the stars, where the Meditation came from. My Letter Slave and Know-It-All lost their influence, but I did appreciate them. Don't they, in their many guises, form the portal to freedom?

Encouraged by the General Secretary of the Anthroposophical Society in The Netherlands, who took the initiative for the Dutch translation of the Esoteric School, I have quoted a number of passages from [the English translation referred to above] in this collection. There are good reasons for this, because the Foundation Stone Meditation is in fact also the foundation of these esoteric lessons. The Foundation Stone was given at the foundation of the worldwide Anthroposophical Society, and at that time the Society also received the task to form an Esoteric School. Already six weeks later Rudolf Steiner gave the first esoteric lesson. If we compare the Foundation Stone with the seed of a tree, then this esoteric cycle is the now fully grown tree. For these are texts with germinal power, particularly if they grow in the ground of the heart, protected and safeguarded by the path of veneration.

Especially because of the publication of these esoteric passages, I have at the beginning of the series of quoted contemplations taken Rudolf Steiner's words on the *path of veneration*, followed by a passage from the Esoteric School about how, when human beings speak and listen, among *Angeloi, Archangeloi, Archai,* a choir of angels' voices sounds in the human soul. Thus the very first call *Human soul!* brings us in conversation with these Angeloi, Archangeloi, and Archai. You can also call them Angels, Archangels, and Primal Beginnings, but whatever you call them, initially all the names of the angels seem abstract. In addition, the word *angels* is, on the one hand, a general term for all the angelic hierarchies but, on the other hand, also the actual name of the hierarchy that is closest to the human being, and which can light up in our thinking power because Angels are themselves thinking powers. This distinction between the two meanings of the word *angeloi (angels)* is as old as ancient esoteric Christianity.

Angels are thinking powers

What are angels? Their Greek name *Angeloi* tells us a lot: *messengers.* Of all spiritual beings they are closest to humanity. Imagine that you want to begin something new. The Archai then join you with ideas. When you talk about the idea with others who also become interested, the Archangels share in it at the feeling level. But the plan also has to be thought through, clarified, and expressed in words; that is when you get the help of the Angels. For that reason the Angels are called "thinking powers," but in this little example you can already see feeling and will power behind thinking power.

The higher worlds are much closer to us than we think. Sometimes you can sense it. In a good conversation in which mutual interest, understanding, and respect are flourishing, you can, for instance, see how your own attention opens itself to the other, and that the other also opens himself to you. Souls open themselves. You can then already sense something of another world. And if in the process you can distinguish between your thinking, feeling, and will, you have made an important next step in getting to know your soul. And if you should succeed in observing those differences in the other, too, you could also see how the thinking, feeling, and will of both of you weave through each other like waves and work and play into each other. That would bring you a big step ahead in your search for the secrets of the human soul.

According to Rudolf Steiner and many others who can concretely see these things, the entire hierarchy of Angels, Archangels and Archai is involved in a good conversation. In the silences during the conversation they can participate with fruitful images, inspirations and ideas. The Angels live in ourselves and in our interlocutor, and also between us. All of this lives already in the first words of the Foundation Stone Meditation: Human soul!

The higher worlds are much closer to us than we think. Sometimes you can sense it. In a good conversation in which mutual interest, understanding, and respect are flourishing, you can, for instance, see how your own attention opens itself to the other, and that the other also opens himself to you.

Souls open themselves.

You can then already sense something of another world.

Now, I have written here the names of the angelic hierarchy that is closest to us as if it is perfectly clear what all this involves. Rudolf Steiner said it with down-to-earth, almost commonplace words:

> Take a thought, for instance—something that lives in a human mind. Initially thoughts exist in our conscious mind, but not only there. Spirits belonging to the next higher hierarchy, Angeloi or Angels, also have that thought. But whereas we have a single thought, the whole of our thought world is a thought of the Angels. The Angels think our conscious mind.

Rudolf Steiner made it sound so simple and direct. But who are those beings in that first hierarchy above us? We see images of Angels in museums, books, periodicals, icons, greeting cards, and on the internet. But we would make a serious error if, even in our dreams, we would view such pictures as reality. And yet, take a beautiful picture of an Angel and try to imagine how it was made. Perhaps the artist had been waiting in a devoted mood for an inspiration that served as the beginning of the picture. Or perhaps works of other great masters had worked as inspirations. If the work was done with loving devotion as well as with knowledge and concentration, angelic voices have worked as inspirations and imaginations. If we then take the time and quiet to give our attention to the work of art, new angelic voices may be heard in it—unless our common consciousness with Know-It-All, Letter Slave, and Hurry-Upper spoils it all and corrupts the image into a caricature. And that happens all too easily.

Recently I heard how the working of the Angels was described in a subtle picture. A person told me that she was longing for an answer to a question. She fell still. "Then a kind of breath passed by, a thought that was unspoken yet understood." You can let such a picture work in you; it can be most meaningful. But it is an image. Breath and air are images from our material world in which Angels have no part. They are thinking powers, feeling powers, will powers. Or in better words, they live in the dynamic interplay of thinking, feeling, and will. Their voices are sometimes audible, provided we are open to them. That is why in the Foundation Stone Meditation it sounds three times: "May human beings hear it!"

There are many pictures of Angels, and yet they do not look like those pictures. In the early years of Christianity this was clearly understood. Dionysius the Areopagite already wrote: "Angels are thinking powers," they are spiritual beings, and he strictly warned people not to confuse the pictures of Angels with reality. Icons of Angels are indications of their spiritual properties, says Dionysius in *About the Heavenly Hierarchy*:

> ... the feet [indicate] the mobile, quick and nimble, always moving toward the divine [...] and for the lightness of the wings, weightless letting themselves be carried to the highest without any connection with the earth, and by nothing diluted [...] the strength of the eyes means the soft, supple, unresisting, quickly moving, and pure, passion-free openness to the enlightenment of God.

And yet, icons are more than just symbols. No, they don't show us sensory things. And no, they are not symbols for dead, abstract concepts; no, icons point to truly existing spiritual qualities. Spiritual realities are much closer to our thinking than we often assume.

To clarify the above I will take a very simple example, namely Santa Claus. Santa Claus? I view the idea that he doesn't exist as a dumb error. Santa Claus, that is us! He exists in ourselves. Acting Santa Claus comes out of the depths of the soul. A force lives there that stands ready to help others, without self-interest, preferably unnoticed. By far most people are familiar with that capacity of neighborly love. When the other day I fell off my bicycle, people rushed up to me from all sides to help me. A smile and a thank-you sufficed when they left. That force, that helpfulness in the human being really exists, it is a spiritual being that is pictured in many different ways in mythology, legends, and Bible stories. For us it is the ever popular Santa Claus. He is a symbol.

But he is also more than a symbol. He is a force that exhorts you to think of something, a force you can feel in yourself, that generates warmth in you and asks for action. He lets you secretly wrap gifts with a smile on your face. He is a thinking power and seizes your heart and will. Don't say that what you are then thinking and feeling is not true or does not exist. That is nonsense. It certainly does exist! Let me say it openly: your secret little plan to give someone a treat with a gift wakes up in you as a message from your Angel being, this time humorously dressed up as Santa Claus. Behind it hides a spiritual being, a thinking power, who wants to work in the world through love and warmth.

But there is a lot of resistance. On the way from the spirit to the earth your nice little plan is exposed to many dangers. For instance, you may get doubts about your motivation; is it really rooted in love—or perhaps in calculation, duty, self-interest? Is it going to work, or do you stumble over delaying things, laziness, forgetfulness, postal delays, etc.—all of them spiritual beings of a lower order that pollute the way to the earth. The good intentions of the good man on the roof right away run into the soot of the chimney.

People who do not understand the spiritual significance of these kinds of humorous pictures won't understand much of the angelic hierarchies, or of mythological and Biblical images such as the spirit in the form of a dove, the god as the protecting eagle, Greek Leda and her swan, Cupid with his arrow, Egyptian Horus as a falcon, etc. Truly existing high spiritual beings appear to us disguised in these kinds of pictures. We have to unveil them ourselves through our own thinking capacity.

Angels are living thinking powers!
Sometimes they appear
as concepts, sometimes as insights,
then again as inspirations
that give us wings, also
as dream pictures or suggestions, feel-
ings that let thoughts grow
in us and lead us to action.

But unfortunately, the awkward part is that we so often perceive our thinking capacities merely in the abstract form of dead thoughts, without awakening the voices of the Angels around us to life. Angels are living thinking powers! Sometimes they appear as concepts, sometimes as insights, then again as inspirations that give us wings, also as dream pictures or suggestions, feelings that let thoughts grow in us and lead us to action. Although you can't see them, they exist. They dwell in the human soul.

You live in your body

Each of the first three panels of the Foundation Stone begins with an aspect of the body—the limbs in space, heart and lungs in rhythm, the head in rest. It sounds like a riddle, and that is indeed what it is. The limbs are a miracle to begin with, hard bones with muscles, flowing blood full of combustible oxygen. The beat of heart and lung—this remarkable rhythm between heart and lungs. And the resting head—not at all easy to bring it actual rest. All of this made from solid matter, liquid, oxygen, warmth, and brought to life by mysterious life forces. Without life forces the body would immediately die.

But what are life forces? Just take a look at an apple in a tree, or a tree full of apples. Physics has the explanation of how the apples fall down, but don't ask them how the apples got up there in the tree. Simplistic explanations such as "turgor" and "electromagnetics" are technical fantasies. The forces of the sphere of life are at work there. When you focus your attention on them you can recognize them. These are the forces that work in water, wherever water creates its own organs. Its own organs in which water can flow up and down as the stream of sap in plants and trees.

Normally, water always flows down. Just look at streams, rivers, rain, and the kitchen faucet. But when water comes alive it wants to go up! That shows you the etheric forces of water, in which the angelic hierarchy of living nature, the Kyriotetes, Dynameis, and Exousiai, work and weave and bring the water to life. Hence the term *spirits' ocean-being* in the Foundation Stone Meditation. People who know the sea know how it is alive in ever-changing movements.

Life is everywhere, also in ground water, in the weaving life under the ground and above the ground, where water creates organs for itself to flow up against gravity. But also around the plants and trees that constantly breathe air there is life, and in the atmosphere around the earth where the birds breathe, in the whole life sphere of the earth, there is life although we don't see it.

The air too creates its own organs. In the world of plants the air still works completely from the outside to bring in the necessary oxygen, rain, and energy. But then comes the change. Air forms its own organs, lungs, an inner world of its own to be able to inhale air. Lungs are connected with their own blood circulation, metabolism, limbs, and internally generated movements. The animals show us these unique movements in marvelous ways, each species in its own slowly evolving, remarkably characteristic ways. See how fiercely a dog attacks another dog, how quietly a cow lies there chewing its cud, how pompously a peacock is showing off, how majestically a flock of birds flies by high in the sky. These are just some examples from close around us, but documentaries also show us the exciting, surprising and magical animal world far away.

All the animals, wherever they live in the world, need oxygen and therefore have lungs, or gills for fishes, thanks to that astonishing capacity of the air to separate itself off and create its own organs, with respiration, senses, blood circulation, and movement. For air and light are blessed with other cosmic forces, astral forces, in which the angelic hierarchies, especially the hierarchy of the Kyriotetes, Dynameis, and Exousiai, work.

And all of this is also true for the human being, for we also bear the laws of the world of plants and animals in us. We, too, are created, supported, and carried by the active forces of the Second Hierarchy. We are therefore also animals. That we are animals, naked apes, we can read in every newspaper. Indeed, don't our never-ending desires and greed lead us to behavior like animals, like predators, one against the other?

And yet, there is a very important and acute difference between humans and animals. Human beings control fire. Animals have in the case of fire no other choice but to run away from it. Humans can make fire serve us, from camp fire to cooking fire, and in all our countless applications and techniques that are dependent on fire in endless different ways. Prometheus stole the fire of the gods from heaven for us humans—a mythological image to ponder deeply. For the fire of the gods is no outer fire. No, the light of the gods, our thinking power, our insight, our capacity to reflect, is divine light with which we have learned to understand and control fire. The development of human culture has made that possible.

According to the Foundation Stone Meditation we owe this inner fire to the "gods' eternal aims"—mysterious words that point to eternity and yet also to the future, just like the name *Prometheus*. In Greek *Prometheus* means: he who has a goal, can think ahead, foresee, which is exactly what you need to control fire. Not only this but, much broader, you receive thinking bestowed on you by the gods' eternal aims "for free and active willing." When using such poignant images, Rudolf Steiner often spoke of "gods," for him usually another word for the angelic hierarchies. It is the Angeloi (Angels) who, as messengers from heaven, light up the light of thinking. Archangeloi (Archangels) bestow on us the love forces they receive from higher hierarchies. And we owe initiative powers to the Archai (Primal Beginnings) which they, in their turn, receive from even higher spheres, and which we can deploy for the world.

When we follow Rudolf Steiner further in his descriptions of the heavenly hierarchies, we see that the third hierarchy is active in human consciousness, while the second hierarchy, which we have in common with the plants and animals, is responsible for the sphere of life. Through the creative thinking powers of the Exousiai we are created. They breathe the breath of life into us and create the stature of our bodies and of all living beings, not only at the time of the Creation in mythical Paradise, but continuously, every day and every minute.

In Rudolf Steiner's terminology, they are called the Spirits of Form. Form arises from movement. Even mathematical forms are thought out of movement. Behind the Spirits of Form, therefore, the Spirits of Movement, the Dynameis, are always working. These are high spiritual beings who receive the movements of the sun, moon, and planets, and the constant movements of the tides, wind, and clouds from the highest hierarchy, and use them to create the sap streams in plants and the blood circulation in humans and animals, daily, in the here and now.

There is something special in the movements and growth forms of living beings. They each have their own character, in which there lives a very specific wisdom. It dwells deep inside them. It is the principle that makes a little child try to become a good person in all respects, and that a sunflower tries to be a beautiful sunflower. Heredity? That is the stream from the past. But here we also witness an inborn striving that works future oriented in the here and now, the force of a wisdom that is anchored in the species and comes into movement in the very first germ, in order to manifest itself in ever-changing forms and characteristic movements. This inborn wisdom is the gift of lofty angelic beings, Kyriotetes; Rudolf Steiner also called them Spirits of Wisdom. They form wisdom, they are the creative will power of wisdom. Every living being show us the longing to bring this spirit of its inner wisdom to expression as much as possible.

Is there really wisdom living in the nature of plants and

animals? Is this wisdom, or are they simply controlled by the laws of heredity and animal behavior? Three observations about this.

First, my description investigates the ordering of the heavenly hierarchies using phenomena everyone can see, purely phenomenologically therefore. Darwin and Mendel, the great researchers of animal behavior and heredity, were formidable phenomenologists. Their observations contain much wisdom. The phenomenological approach to plants and animals and to the starry heaven means: Hold your assumptions and judgments back. We can learn much from this. And it is also the path of veneration.

Second, a few words about a particular interpretation of the Biblical creation story, where it says that the plants and animals were created "according to their kinds," meaning according to the spirit of their inborn wisdom. Unfortunately, rigid theological thinking has led to the idea that their nature was fixed for eternity and could not further develop, but that is not what it says there. On the contrary, with a phenomenological view I think I can see myself that the inborn wisdom of a species, the gift of the Kyriotetes, uses the laws of heredity to develop the species further. In the meantime, with gene manipulation and other materialistic techniques the human being is now capable of taking over the position of the Spirits of Wisdom. Kyriotetes are, sometimes with the best of intentions, made subservient to the spirit of greed. And we should fully expect that such an ahrimanic variant of a being of the second hierarchy would then fester on its own. We should be much more careful with Mother Nature.

Third, a brief comment on the Creator, who is described in the Foundation Stone Meditation as "the wielding World-Creator-Being" and "the Father-Spirit of the heights." He performs the ubiquitous creation process by means of the angelic hierarchies, as Rudolf Steiner describes in mighty pictures in his book *An Outline of Esoteric Science*, and indicates extremely briefly in the Foundation Stone by repeatedly invoking a subsequent hierarchy. The hierarchies therefore do not create on their own. One could say that he lets his creative words sound through them. Thus he creates through them—matter through the first hierarchy, the living nature through the second hierarchy, and human consciousness through the third hierarchy.

In the Biblical creation story, God is called in Hebrew *Elohim*, a peculiar plural form, with the accompanying verb always in singular. According to Rudolf Steiner, the Elohim belongs to the Trinity and from there reaches down through the hierarchies into the sphere of the Exousiai. He also calls the Elohim simply Exousiai, and in that role they create the form of each human being as a thought. They offer themselves as elemental beings to the earth, in order to let their fiery footprints work in it. In this way they create our limbs.

Our limbs are problematic beings. I have already mentioned that Ahriman, just as Lucifer, is able to lead even Kyriotetes astray. How much more the human being! Our limbs are fire power; they can be human but also beastly, loaded with desire and aggression. With your limbs you can do anything. Aren't they for the will the portal to the surrounding world? But we are pulled up and down, we strive for the higher or the lower—the choice is ours. In the energy of our limbs hides desire, fear, and aggression on the one hand, but on the other hand also our conscience, our moral ideals. All this we let stream into the world through our limbs. In brief, the word *limbs* takes us into a world of fundamental questions.

Sometimes Rudolf Steiner says it quite schematically. In the physical aspect of the world the working of the highest angelic hierarchy is visible. In living nature works the second hierarchy. The human soul is the stage of the third hierarchy. Then he broadens such a schematic and makes it dynamic so that everything comes into movement. Hardly have you understood that the Angeloi kindle the inner light in our consciousness, and then everything seems different when he says that the Angeloi live in the sun and the sunlight, the light forces in our eyes, and that they thus call our consciousness to life. But indeed, our consciousness is as broad as the divine light which, according to the third panel of the Foundation Stone, we receive bestowed on us "for free and active willing," in the hope that we are then mature enough to follow the light of the poor shepherds and wise kings. Thus lives the light in our consciousness as a gift from the third hierarchy, provided we want to see it.

And yet light is much greater and mightier than our consciousness. Just take a good look at the way light wakes up the plant world in spring; in early spring even under the ground. "Up, up, to the light!" the plants seem to call. Light lives in the movements of the animals, in sun, moon, and stars, and in world rhythms. This is the light of the second hierarchy. It is spoken, called, sung by the Biblical Elohim: "Let there be light!" This light fires us up in the morning; it is the divine light in which we stand from sunrise to sundown, from East to West. But there is also a movement of the sun in the other direction, from West to East through the signs of the zodiac as the working of the first hierarchy. In the quoted contemplations a remarkable description of this by Rudolf Steiner can be found.

Do we now have clear insight into the way light manifests in the three hierarchies? Can we presume that this is also the case with the human I? But Rudolf Steiner is ahead of us again. Now he says that before the creation the light was with the Trinity, from where the Elohim work through into the first, then into the second hierarchy down to the Exousiai. Thus waves and weaves Rudolf Steiner's thinking back and forth between understandable schematics on the one hand, and the sparkling, beaming, pulsating, metamorphosing life in and between them.

Right now, I am seeing through my window how the sunlight plays among the hundreds of budding flowers of a magnolia tree. There is a mysterious wisdom that lives in the magnolia slumbering in the buds all winter, waiting for the right moment

The schematic of the angelic hierarchy is nothing more than a reflection of this hierarchy in human thinking, at a level that earth dwellers can understand. But the schematic still contains wisdom, for we can practice more profound understanding with it.

to appear. Now the light has come. Light bestows on this tree the forces to begin to move, and form flowers, leaves, and fruit. Their growth is movement, cautious movement that becomes visible in successive forms, from leaf to flower, from flower to fruit. Thus we see behind the Spirits of Form the Spirits of Movement, and behind them the Spirits of Wisdom, or behind the Exousiai, the Dynameis, and behind them the Kyriotetes. Have we now caught the second hierarchy in a neat little schematic? Of course not. The schematic is nothing more than a reflection of this hierarchy in human thinking, at a level that earth dwellers can understand. But the schematic still contains wisdom, for we can practice more profound understanding with it.

Maybe it helps if I bring in the memory of a moment when the first hierarchy briefly lit up for me. I was standing in a crystal shop in Switzerland in an area where many crystals are found. There I saw a large, shining, clear crystal showing off its mathematical form, and I thought of a surprising word of Rudolf Steiner from the eleventh lesson of his Esoteric School: *World foundation powers, Radiant love of the Creator.* And there was that crystal, dug out of the depth, out of the sphere of the Creator. I saw the forming power, pure power of form, not only the outside but also deep inside. Matter at its best, a message of the Thrones. And through the entire crystal light quality, pure, harmonious, loving light quality, gift of the Cherubim or Spirits of Harmony, which can sometimes even sound in our personal conscience. Actually we would want to be as pure as a crystal. And then the unique individual character of this crystal showed itself in its unmistakable pointed six-sided form. A line from the Calendar of the Soul occurred to me: *Ich fühle wie verzaubert im Weltenschein des Geistes Weben—I feel the Spirit's weaving as though enchanted in the cosmic glory*—deeply hidden, very high consciousness like life in death.

The crystal forms no sap stream, no blood circulation, such as the second hierarchy can do, but it wants to *be*, purely *be*, and withdraws the necessary minerals directly from its surroundings for this. In the Foundation Stone the Creator is therefore called "begetting life." This is how concretely the working of the Seraphim-Cherubim-Thrones and the gift they bestow on the Kyriotetes can sometimes be visible. Is the crystal now fixed in a schematic? Not at all. Just wait for the mighty workings of the world rhythms of wind, clouds, raging torrents to destroy the crystals. They grind them into gravel or sand.

Then the second hierarchy gets its turn and creates fields filled with mountain flowers, or behind us a magnolia tree in which a blackbird is singing. And we humans hear that, feel it, as long as the third hierarchy bestows on the soul the gift of good listening. Angel choirs in the garden? A schematic? The schematic only has the character of a picture, no real existence. Should we therefore get rid of it? No, we shouldn't. Rudolf Steiner used schematics all the time as simple aids for our thinking consciousness, as a first step toward clarity in the wondrous interplay of the angelic hierarchies.

The world of space

The world of space, what does that mean? In a course about the fourth dimension Rudolf Steiner was asked whether we should picture the working of the angelic hierarchies spatially or independent of space. His answer can be found in the quoted contemplation to the Foundation Stone passage on page 75 of this volume. Among other things he says:

> We should not picture the highest Trinity as spatial, for space is one of its creations. We should imagine [spiritual] beings as existing without space; space is something that was created. But the workings of the hierarchies in our world are spatially limited, like those of human beings. The other hierarchies move therefore within space.

According to *An Outline of Esoteric Science* the activities of the hierarchies begin with the Old Saturn phase, in which the Thrones form a space with their warmth of which we are only somewhat reminded by the orbit of Saturn. This means that the awesome development described there takes place within the space of our own planetary system. Rudolf Steiner describes this space as a hallowed, living space filled with the workings of the divine World Word that sounds forth through the angelic hierarchies.

In the meantime the popular image of the earth has undergone rapid development. The first pictures of our planet taken from the moon still give us the impression of a unique etheric being, our homeland, our only earth that makes a moral appeal on us to take good care of it. These more and more perfect pictures from the period 1968–1972 marked the beginning of our environmental consciousness. They are pictures of the earth that emanate a moral appeal. We came to view our earth as the only conceivable one, "round and blue in space."

In 2022, half a century later, we started seeing totally different pictures of space. The James Webb telescope is now hanging between sun and earth on some point of balance, quietly moving with us. The great space researchers use it to search for the first light, the big bang, the moment or point from which the all-encompassing cohesion of the cosmos may be understood. They try to fathom the first light. The telescope has generated amazing pictures of space, with thousands of star systems playing through a fantastic space. First you think that you are looking at a big piece of space, but that isn't true. Just hold a scrap of paper with a pinprick at arms length. Then look through the hole to heaven. That way you see exactly how small the piece of cosmic space is that is shown in the first published photograph of the James Webb telescope. Through that pinprick you see an infinitely large space full of countless, repeat countless Milky Ways.

When this picture was personally shared with the media by the President it made an indelible impression. Worldwide the public was confronted with a totally new view of space. Everyone, all students, all school children will from now on be educated with these pictures. My grandchildren talk about it with enthusiasm. Just search "pictures James Webb" on the internet and you know: Is the earth our only planet? Not at all! There are millions of planets with water and living beings! Some day we will be able to travel to them! Lots of technical fantasy. Still, the great space researchers assume that the laws of physics they work with also held true fourteen billion years ago at the extreme boundary of space. They are not interested in the pictures but only in the laws of physics they read in them, pure computations that would therefore also be valid for the first light. At any rate, they are searching for the first light, along the way out into the cosmos.

The way in is no less fascinating. Enormous amounts of money are spent for research into the most inner inside of matter, of molecules, atoms, elementary particles, quarks, quants, etc., the incomprehensibly complex and mobile whole of interacting forces. But all students, all school children, all other people who are looking for knowledge of atoms in school books and computer screens, see as representations of atoms virtually nothing but schematic pictures of little globes that revolve around each other—a totally misleading materialistic picture that has taken root deeply in our thinking, all over the world. Real atom scientists know better. They view atoms not as little globes but as interacting forces of which they imagine that they can be purely mathematically computed, and with which they could possibly unravel the enigma of the first light.

During my preparations for this book I found a passage of Rudolf Steiner in which he deals with this difference in viewing atoms. He was an absolute opponent of the idea that atoms are little globes of matter. Rather, he views a purely mathematical model of atoms as a first step in the direction of a more spiritual view of matter:

> It is pure fantasy to take the existence of atoms, as envisaged today, to be real. So long as atoms are looked upon merely as counters or shorthand notes for what the senses actually show, we keep our feet on the ground. If we want to penetrate behind the sense-perceptible layer, however, we have to rise to the realm of the spirit, where we reach the living movement of a basic substance which is none other than the bodily nature of the Thrones, permeated by the activity of the Spirits of Form [Exousiai].

Scientifically, atoms have not been viewed as little globes for a long time, but as mathematical entities. Be that as it may, no matter how we look for a graphic or mathematical concept of matter and space, it will never help us to know ourselves. The great call that sounded from the Greek mysteries, the call "Know yourself"—which is actually included in the very first word of the Foundation Stone Meditation—this call opens the way to the light within ourselves, the light in our heart, past all angelic hierarchies up to our most hallowed expectations, where the Christ will works through the world, blessing souls, warming hearts, and enlightening heads.

After this introduction about veneration, the working of the angels, and space, I want to leave as much as possible—everything really—to everyone's personal discoveries in the texts of Rudolf Steiner. Let it suffice that his texts are always quoted in relation to particular thoughts of the Foundation Stone Meditation.

But there are two points I still need to mention. First, the structure of the Foundation Stone as a whole, leading to the riddle of why Rudolf Steiner repeatedly called the Foundation Stone Meditation a *dodecahedron.* Second, the harmonious ordering of the angelic world into three hierarchies, each consisting of three groups of angels, this ordering that is manifested in the Foundation Stone and in all of anthroposophy—where does it come from? And what is its significance in the work of Rudolf Steiner?

The structure of the Foundation Stone Meditation

The inner order of the Foundation Stone is an amazing open secret. This is especially noticeable when we can oversee the four panels at a glance.

Through the first three panels we feel the waves of threefoldness. First we are led from our limbs to our heart-lung rhythm and to our resting head; that refers to the threefoldness of our body. That is the well-known threefoldness of head, heart, and hands, recognizable for everyone.

Then the text names what surrounds our body: the world of space, experienced on earth as length, breadth, and height; the rhythms of time that we experience as past, present, and future; and finally eternity, the sphere of the divine Trinity.

Thereupon the text indicates how we can open ourselves to the spirit, again in three ways: the limbs open themselves for "the spirits' ocean-being," the sphere of life, the etheric. In rhythms the heart-lung movement opens itself to the soul feeling as a living being. And the resting head opens itself to world thoughts.

But Rudolf Steiner does not leave us in peace. Now come the exercises: practice-practice-practice! After all, that is anthroposophy. The first exercise is of memory, focused on the past therefore. The second is the art of balancing all the dazzling and stupendous developments of the here and now. The last exercise looks to the future, "the god's eternal aims." This exercise takes place in the spirit, when our thoughts have come to rest. To this point the text is crystal clear.

But now things become a little more difficult. Perhaps the

simplest thing to do to enhance our understanding is to go to the Latin mottos of the Rosicrucians that are said to have been found in 1604 in the grave of Christian Rosenkreutz. Since the Anthroposophical Congress of 1907 Rudolf Steiner often referred to these three mottos, sometimes using only the first letter of each word, such as on the title page of his four Mystery Dramas. And he translated the mottos in many different variants.

When the Foundation Stone was laid he spoke the three mottos in Latin. The first sounded: "Ex Deo nascimur," literally: "Out of God we are born." It reflects an old thought that goes back to the Biblical creation story. It asks us to raise our gaze from the created to the Creator. Everywhere around us, and in ourselves, we can see the Creator at work, from the beginning, and therefore even now: "Out of God we are born." If we hold on to this we can go back to the point where we left off in the text, connecting with the three exercises focused on past, present and future.

First we read that in the mighty world-creator-being our own I "comes into being in the I of God." Doesn't that mean in different words the same as the Latin motto: Out of God we are born? The text continues: "The Father-Spirit of the heights holds sway in depths of worlds begetting life." Isn't that for the second time the same thought: the Father Spirit is our creator? Now we hear it in Latin: "Ex Deo nascimur." The content of the motto sounds for the third time.

In the second panel we see something similar. There sounds the second Rosicrucian saying: *In Christo morimur*, literally translated: "In Christ we die." The motto goes back to early esoteric Christianity. Then already dying in Christ was understood as resurrection, not only at the moment of our physical death, but also during our life, at the birth of the "second human being" in us of which Paul speaks: "I am crucified with Christ. So it is not I who live, but Christ lives in me" (Gal. 2:20). It happened to him when his name was still Saul, on the way to Damascus.

New light enters every time we decide to get rid of old junk, to have a spring cleaning. Then we make room to receive forces that "bestow grace upon souls."

He was overwhelmed by an experience of light, felt as if dead, was baptized, received the name Paul, and began a new life. He called himself a "second human being." He felt dead and born in Christ. This is an example of the resurrection during life, in the greatest possible form.

But there are also countless smaller examples. My physiotherapist told me recently that soon after his graduation from high school he barely survived a terrible accident with his scooter. Years of revalidation eventually put him on his feet again. Looking back he said: "I wouldn't have missed it. I put my whole life upside down. All my norms and values are different now!" It just shows that even during normal life the "second human being" can break into your life like a thief in the night.

It might just as well happen that the second, or spiritual, human being announces himself in little daily things in our life, for example, in the power of forgiveness. Suppose that after many dreary years of endless resentment you forgive the person who had done you an injustice. Your imprisonment in the role of the victim is then dead, and you can begin a new life! You experience a little bit of resurrection. New light enters every time we decide to get rid of old junk, to have a spring cleaning. Then we make room to receive forces that "bestow grace upon souls."

In early Christianity it was felt that the imitation of Christ began with the baptism. The baptism was the decision to go to church daily or weekly, where people would hear examples from the life of Jesus for many years. In this way the Church had an enormous moral effect, also on small children who were already taken to church by their parents or caregivers when they were still very young and were brought up in the spirit of the Gospel.

Of course, I know, church is only as good as its people. It is unfortunately corrupted. All conceivable kinds of abuse have happened, but that was not the intention of the early church as beacon of care for one's neighbor at the time of a disintegrating Roman Empire that had itself become totally corrupt. And if we want to understand the good intentions of the early Church—and of honorable people later—we first have to understand the oldest Church and its inspiration from esoteric Christianity. For then already the baptism was understood as letting the old egoistic, greedy life die, in order to begin a new life. "Dying" at the baptism meant to step into a new life guided by Christ. But this "being born in Christ" doesn't just happen—people were fully aware of that. It was viewed as a lifelong battle with the dark powers in yourself, with the help of Christ. This was symbolized by the threefold immersion and rising up again from the water—a threefold mystery: birth from God, resurrection in Christ, and union with the Spirit. This was the practice in early esoteric Christianity, and thus it was written down by Dionysius in Greek around 500 AD. And thus this mystery was summarized in a Latin motto by the Rosicrucians more than a thousand years later.

We are now living in different times. The baptism is experienced as a mere ritual, not a threefold mystery. That is no longer possible in our time of the consciousness soul. If we want to take a spiritual path we will have to do it ourselves by choosing a spiritual path of schooling and following it consciously. And yet, ordinary life is also a path of schooling, particularly if you strive for real ideals, for instance, when you fight for care of the earth. That is a path of learning too. Among all the possibilities anthroposophy is a conscious choice that can certainly be a threefold mystery.

When we regularly meditate on the Foundation Stone text we let something new be born in us in the presence of the spirit. A second, a spiritual entity then grows in the human being. You are reborn just as Jesus said to Nicodemus during the night: You have to be born from water and the Spirit, words with which He held up His own baptism in the Jordan as an example. All the wonderful pictures of that baptism show it: the spirit as a dove above Him, the water of the river below Him. He is "born anew," the old human being dies. Rudolf Steiner's rendition of *In Christo morimur* is therefore entirely to the point: "In Christ death becomes life." It is completely in line with ancient esoteric Christianity.

The second panel of the Foundation Stone takes us from the world of space to processes in time: "rhythms of time," "surging deeds of world-evolving," "the human soul's creating," "the beat of heart and lung." Rudolf Steiner discussed the relationship of all of this with the planetary rhythms in beautiful passages; perhaps I should say "celebrated" because it is about Christ as Lord of the working of the sun and the rhythms of the planets. And it is also about Christ who "bestows grace upon souls," not only in death but also already now—letting something old die and something new be born. Three times it sounds in the second panel. First we are "united" with the world-I, Christ. Then he "bestows grace upon us." And finally sounds the three-part choir which unites us with Him for the third time: *In Christo morimur.*

The third panel of the Foundation Stone puts us into a different mood again, even into another dimension. After the dimensions of space and time, here reign pure eternity, stillness of thought, eternal aims. It is the sphere in which birth and death no longer have an essential significance, the sphere of the Holy Spirit who accompanies us through our successive incarnations. The third Rosicrucian saying testifies to this: *Per Spiritum Sanctum reviviscimus*, literally translated: *Through the Holy Spirit we are reborn.*

These words are first prepared by bestowing the light of cosmic being on our own I. In the second step we implore light, which leads the angels to speak in us when we pray what in the heights can be heard. In a third step we hear the choir of Archai, Archangeloi, and Angeloi: *Per Spiritum Sanctum reviviscimus.*

The Rosicrucian sayings appear in three times three steps.

Three parts with their resplendent, astonishing content in a lucid, ninefold structure.

The fourth panel completes the picture. That panel too is threefold: the turning point of time brings us into the cosmic dimension of the "gods' eternal aims," for the descent of Christ to the earth was, according to Rudolf Steiner, part of our planetary development from the beginning. That is the cosmic dimension. Then follows the historical dimension, here indicated by the mention of the poor shepherds' hearts and the wise heads of kings at the time when Christ came to the earth. And finally, what we direct with our will, by definition focused on the future. The will still slumbers in the world-I in the first panel; then, in spirit sensing, is integrated in balance of the soul in the second panel; and in the third panel receives its thinking as a promise for the free will. Finally, at the end of the meditation it is addressed in its fullness in "what we direct with focused will." For those present at the time this was the founding of the Society, but now it refers to our conscious will that looks into the future and hopes for the help of Christ in taking and leading initiatives. Thus we also see three dimensions in the fourth panel. The Foundation Stone is complete: four panels, each with three qualities, twelve together.

We can also discover another dodecahedron in the Foundation Stone. It shows when we don't direct our attention to the ninefold angelic hierarchy in the Rosicrucian saying, but to body, soul, and spirit as threefoldness. For the first three panels of the Foundation Stone are oriented first on the body—"you live within the limbs," etc.—then on the soul, with the exercises for the soul, and finally on the spirit, from the Father Spirit to the spirits of the elements. In the first panel this threefoldness appears in the world of space, then in the rhythms of time, and finally in the eternity of the third panel—all together, therefore, in nine aspects. Including the three dimensions of the last panel, the four panels thus show us twelve facets.

From this point of view, attention has moved to the threefoldness of body, soul, and spirit, which is a fundamental aspect of anthroposophy. But the accent is then no longer on the ninefoldness of the Rosicrucian sayings that sound in the Foundation Stone, nor on the ninefold ordering of the angelic hierarchies as the foundation of anthroposophy.

These points of view seem different, but are they really? Or are they in essence the same? In his book *An Outline of Esoteric Science*, Rudolf Steiner characterized body, soul, and spirit as the work of the first, second, and third hierarchies in the human being. The above contemplations about the twelvefold aspect of the Foundation Stone therefore stand in living interplay close together. We see this interplay immediately at the beginning of each panel: "You live within..." and in the last panel: "Entered the stream..." That is interaction, interplay, balance, exactly what the Foundation Stone emanates all the time. And thus there is also an intimate exchange between the two perspectives on the Foundation Stone as dodecahedron mentioned above.

Finally, let us realize briefly that a dodecahedron consists of pentagons. Are these recognizable in the four panels of the Foundation Stone? The first panel has, as it were, five players, five angles: the limbs, the human soul in depths of soul, the Father-Spirit, the angelic hierarchies, and the spirits of the elements. These five go through metamorphoses in the subsequent panels. And we can observe this fivefold order also in the grammatical structure of the Foundation Stone.

In 1913 Rudolf Steiner caused a physical charter to be enclosed in the Foundation Stone for the first Goetheanum. The Foundation Stone consisted of two dodecahedrons, two regularly shaped spatial forms of twelve pentagons each, one larger with the other, smaller one fit onto it, the whole made of copper. On the charter a sketch of the same double dodecahedron was drawn with the initials of the three Rosicrucian sayings. Apparently Rudolf Steiner had even then realized the dodecahedric quality of the Rosicrucian sayings.

After the burning of the first Goetheanum Rudolf Steiner did not lay a new physical foundation stone for the worldwide Society, but instead the foundation was laid in the form of a meditation in the hearts and souls of the 800 attending founders: the Foundation Stone Meditation. The first morning of the conference he characterized it seven times as a dodecahedron. We may understand the Foundation Stone as having twelve purely regular pentagons, as a dodecahedron.

The ordering of the angelic hierarchies

In his book *An Outline of Esoteric Science*, the hierarchies of the angels play a fundamental role. The structure of the hierarchies is not conspicuous because Rudolf Steiner uses a variety of different descriptive names for the spiritual beings. As a result, the living, burgeoning character of the angelic world stands out so strongly that the basic division into first, second, and third hierarchy recedes somewhat into the background. But it received more emphasis in the lecture series Rudolf Steiner gave for members when he was writing this book. In these lectures he used almost consistently the Greek names of the nine groups of angels, as a result of which the basic structure is more easily recognizable.

We can find this structure almost everywhere in Rudolf Steiner's books and lectures. The third hierarchy creates our consciousness, the second creates living nature including our body, the first creates the mineral world in its four elements, which of course also occur in our body. In all of this the hierarchies create and make use of elemental beings in a surprising, ever-changing and renewing, living and warming, and love-seeking development, while overcoming the powers of adversaries.

When we pay close attention, the basic structure always remains visible in this development. Random samples and estimates tell me that the angelic hierarchies are mentioned at least 10 or 20 times in some 200 volumes of Rudolf Steiner collected works, in total perhaps 3000 times. I don't care about the exact number, but about the realization of how fundamentally the concept of the hierarchies has been anchored in Rudolf Steiner's work as a teaching with a firm structure that is fully alive and in an all-encompassing development.

What was the origin of this teaching of the hierarchies? Rudolf Steiner was crystal clear about this: it goes back to early esoteric Christianity, specifically to the apostle Paul who initiated his student Dionysius the Areopagite into esoteric Christianity and appointed him as leader of an esoteric school. Rudolf Steiner presumed that the successors of this Dionysius all adopted the name of Dionysius, and that the last Dionysius wrote this teaching down centuries later. Perhaps this was a supersensory reality, for nowhere, absolutely nowhere in the literature of the time can we find any trace of such a school. The current view is that the unknown Dionysius—his text emerged in 529 AD— posed as the first Dionysius as a literary trick, for which all kinds of possible reasons are fabricated. Recently we have also been hearing a different sound. The possibility is suggested that the last Dionysius identified himself so strongly with the first, Paul's follower, that he really began to feel as if he was Dionysius, the follower of Paul. Had he perhaps intuitively seen what Paul experienced in "the third heavenly sphere" (2 Cor. 12:2)? Be this as it may, Rudolf Steiner mentioned the name Dionysius in 34 volumes of his collective works, and most of the time he put the question of his mysterious identity aside. All he said was that Dionysius "structured" the hierarchies. That seems rather rigid—which it is indeed. But Rudolf Steiner wouldn't be Rudolf Steiner if he didn't put such a strict teaching into movement. And that is precisely what he did in *An Outline of Esoteric Science.*

In the meantime, 700 years after Dionysius' text and 700 years before Rudolf Steiner, the great theologian-philosopher Thomas Aquinas appeared on the scene. As an extremely wise scholar this Thomas dominated the philosophy of the Catholic Church for centuries. He made the angelic hierarchies of Dionysius into one of the cornerstones of the faith. It is said that he quoted Dionysius 1700 times in his works. Although Dionysius also had great influence in the School of Chartres a hundred years earlier, Thomas was still considered to be the greatest Dionysius interpreter—until Rudolf Steiner appeared. Steiner mentioned Dionysius' teaching of the hierarchies even more often than Thomas and made it into a cornerstone of his spiritual science.

Now, when I compare the texts of Dionysius, Thomas, and Steiner I think I can say the following. Dionysius "structured" the hierarchies at the level of the intellectual soul. Thomas translated them according to the faith, so that the pious faithful could take the imaginations of the angelic world into their heart and feelings. Rudolf Steiner went further to the creative will. He revealed the creative role of the angelic hierarchies implementing the divine will of the Trinity in the great developmental phases of the universe, but also in the human body. Steiner revealed himself as knowing Dionysius at least as well as Thomas Aquinas.

But he did not merely copy this teaching. The autonomous manner in which Steiner approached the teaching of Dionysius, transformed and developed it, is, in my view, an indication that he knew these things not only from Dionysius' texts, but that he could see them directly from his own spiritual-scientific research. He gave an indication in this direction in a unique statement about "pre-creational divine thoughts." These are the actual words in the English language edition: *pre-creational divine thoughts*, which he attributed to Thomas and Dionysius and to which, as appears from the text, he also had access. I quote:

> The scholastic system was the most perfect web of logic, and it enabled Thomas to think anew the pre-creational divine thoughts, freed from error and delusion as they can be conceived of only in monastic seclusion far away from the noise of the world.
>
> Human beings are eager to comprehend quickly, to adopt an idea and make it their own, and to simplify everything. But the divine is not that simple! With Thomas Aquinas, human thought rises to new heights. Being no less a mystic than a scholastic, Thomas was able to give us such vivid descriptions, similar to those of the seer Dionysius the Areopagite, because he saw the spiritual hierarchies and thus he was able to solve the most difficult problems during his long nightly meditations in front of the altar. Therefore, we find combined in him the qualities of a mystic and of a brilliant thinker who is not influenced by the senses.

Let this profound statement suffice. Rudolf Steiner mentioned the name of Dionysius altogether in forty places, but it exceeds the purpose of this introduction to pursue this. Steiner's modern spiritual-scientific teaching regarding the hierarchies shows countless similarities with the old esoteric teaching, as he repeatedly said himself: thoughts from before the creation, in an old esoteric Christian form but in essence the same as anthroposophy.

The philosophical aspect of the Rosicrucian sayings

To conclude this introduction, I want to go into the philosophical parallel of the Rosicrucian sayings in Greek philosophy. To make this clear I will first quote Rudolf Steiner about the path of incarnation from the spirit to the earth, and the path of excarnation from the earth to the spirit:

> And exalted above both, above being born and dying, there is a third principle that comes from both, and is equally related to both the divine Father and the divine Son: the Spirit, the Holy Spirit. Thus we can recognize in the human being:
>
> the transition from the supersensory to the sensory: *Ex Deo nascimur*
>
> the transition from the sensory into the supersensory: *In Christo morimur*, and
>
> the union of both, the connection with that in which neither birth nor death have true significance anymore, the awakening by the Spirit: *Per Spiritum Sanctum reviviscimus.*

The descent of Christ to the earth is in the view of Rudolf Steiner a process of cosmic dimensions, which was supersensibly observed by other religions and streams, long before His arrival on earth. This was also the case in Greek culture, where the Rosicrucian sayings were already being prepared as philosophical thoughts hundreds of years before the descent of Christ to the earth. Indeed, in pre-Christian times the great thought was already known in Greek philosophy that Rudolf Steiner attached to the Rosicrucian sayings for better understanding, a thought that has a long history in Greek philosophy.

The point of departure is that the godhead, the One, is the cause of everything. This cause remains forever. Out of this point of departure the godhead steps forward and manifests himself in everything observable through the senses. The stepping forward of the godhead is *prohodos*. Everything originates in the One, the one cause of all, and therefore harbors the longing to return to the One. Return is *epistrophè*. Every object and every living being that possesses unity and structure originates in the One who lasts, longs back to the One, is part of the One, as long as it is a being, whether living or not. Whatever possesses unity and structure is a being, and as long as that is what it is, it shares in what lasts: *menein.*

In a thousand years of Greek philosophy this thought has played a role. The great philosopher Proclus, a Neo-Platonist who was initiated in the mysteries of Orpheus, uniquely summarized it as the ripe fruit of Neo-Platonism. He was not a Christian, in contrast to his somewhat younger contemporary Dionysius. The latter recognized—in the footprints of Clemens of Alexandria—the same thought in the religious images of the Bible: The Eternal One from whom we have come forth and to whom we long to return, Christ, is the beginning and the end, *Alpha and Omega.* Resurrection in Christ makes the return possible, the transcendence of the old philosophical thought in the reality of the resurrection. Pentecost celebrates the flaming up of the Spirit as the lasting core of the human being. For Dionysius this was all part of the nocturnal conversation between Jesus and Nicodemus about being reborn "from water and the spirit," which is the baptism in which our descent from the spiritual world to the earth, our ascent out of the sphere of the earth to the spirit, and our eternal spiritual core are recapitulated in a single sacrament.

Thus this great, all-encompassing thought can be approached in two ways: in philosophical language as *prohodos—epistrophè—menein*, and in religious images that are summarized in the Rosicrucian sayings. But, in truth, this fundamental thought is the same in philosophical language as in religious language:

> *Ex Deo nascimur – In Christo morimur – Per Spiritum Sanctum reviviscimus.*

Angels Speak

The Foundation Stone Meditation

Contemplations for the First Panel

THE PATH OF VENERATION

In a conversation about the concept of this book, someone suggested shortening the first passage, the part about the path of veneration. He wrote: "What I as a reader find complicated is that almost right away there is a longer text from Knowledge of the Higher Worlds. *It distracts me. Is it possible to shorten these texts somewhat and get more quotations from them to highlight what you want to say about this part?" I did my best to follow this suggestion. I reflected that he was right because I recognized also in myself the tendency to rush over things. Are we still able to produce time and attention for a three-page passage about veneration? And precisely because I recognized that tendency in myself to rush things it became impossible to shorten the text about the path of veneration or leave it out! It simply stood there: "A certain fundamental attitude of soul" has to be the beginning. For the path of veneration is the portal to the angels' voices that will sound in all the subsequent Contemplations for the words of the Foundation Stone Meditation in their full riches. Therefore, first comes the path of reverence, which could also inwardly sound through all subsequent fragments.*

Rudolf Steiner, *Knowledge of the Higher Worlds* (CW 10), Chapter 1:

We begin with a fundamental mood of soul. Spiritual researchers call this basic attitude *the path of reverence*, of devotion to truth and knowledge. Only those who have acquired this fundamental mood or attitude can become pupils in an esoteric school. Anyone with any experience in this area knows that those who later become students of esoteric knowledge demonstrate this gift for reverence in childhood. Some children look up to those whom they revere with a holy awe. Their profound respect for these people works into the deepest recesses of their hearts and forbids any thought of criticism or opposition to arise. Such people grow up into young people who enjoy looking up to something that fills them with reverence. Many of these young people become students of esoteric knowledge.

If you have ever stood before the door of someone you revered, filled with holy awe as you turned the doorknob to enter for the first time a room that was a "holy place" for you, then the feeling you experienced at that moment is the seed that can later blossom into your becoming a student in an occult, esoteric school. To be gifted with the potential for such feelings is a blessing for every young person.

We should not fear that such feelings for reverence lead to subservience and slavery; on the contrary, a child's reverence for others develops into a reverence for truth and knowledge. Experience teaches that we know best how to hold our heads high in freedom if we have learned to feel reverence when it is appropriate—and it is appropriate whenever it flows from the depths of the heart.

We will not find the inner strength to evolve to a higher level if we do not inwardly develop this profound feeling that there is something higher than ourselves. Initiates found the strength to lift themselves to the heights of knowledge only because they first guided their hearts into the depths of veneration and devotion. Only a person who has passed through the gate of humility can ascend to the heights of the spirit. To attain true knowledge, you must first learn to respect this knowledge.

We certainly have the right to turn our eyes toward the light, but we must earn this right. Spiritual life has its laws just as physical life does. Rub a glass rod with the appropriate substance and it becomes electrified—that is, the glass rod will now have the power to attract small particles. This process demonstrates a physical law. If one has learned some elementary physics, one knows that this is so. Similarly, if one knows the fundamentals of esoteric science, one knows that every feeling of *true* devotion unfolded in the soul produces an inner strength or force that sooner or later leads to knowledge.

Whoever possesses an innate tendency toward feelings of devotion, or has been lucky enough to receive an education that cultivated those feelings, is well prepared in later life to seek the way to higher knowledge. Those who do not bring this preparation with them will have to work at developing this devotional mood with vigorous self-discipline; if not, they will encounter difficulties after taking only the first few steps on the path of knowledge. In our time it is particularly important to focus complete attention on this point. Our civilization is more inclined to criticize, judge, and condemn than to feel devotion and selfless veneration. Our children criticize far more than they respect or revere. But just as surely as every feeling of devotion and reverence nurtures the soul's powers for higher knowledge, so every act of criticism and judgment drives these powers away.

This is not meant to imply anything against our civilization—our concern here is not to criticize it. After all, we owe the greatness of our culture precisely to our ability to make critical, self-confident human judgments and to our principle of "testing all and keeping the best." Modern science, industry, transportation, commerce, law—all these would never have developed without the universal exercise of our critical faculty and standards of judgment. But the price of this gain in outer culture has been a corresponding loss in higher knowledge and spiritual life. Therefore we must never forget that higher knowledge has to do with revering truth and insight and not with revering people.

Nevertheless, we must be clear about one thing. Those

completely immersed in the superficial civilization of our day will find it particularly difficult to work their way to cognition of the higher worlds. To do so, they will have to work energetically upon themselves. In times when the material conditions of life were still simple, spiritual progress was easier. What was revered and held sacred stood out more clearly from the rest of the world. In the age of criticism, on the other hand, ideals are degraded. Reverence, awe, adoration, and wonder are replaced by other feelings—they are pushed more and more into the background. As a result, everyday life offers very few opportunities for their development. Anyone seeking higher knowledge must create these feelings inwardly, instilling them in the soul. This cannot be done by studying. It can be done only by living.

If we wish to become esoteric students, we must train ourselves vigorously in the mood of devotion. We must seek—in all things around us, in all our experiences—for what can arouse our admiration and respect. If I meet other people and criticize their weaknesses, I rob myself of higher cognitive power. But if I try to enter deeply and lovingly into another person's good qualities, I gather in that force.

Disciples of this occult path must always bear in mind the need to cultivate such admiration and respect. Experienced spiritual researchers know what strength they gain by always looking for the good in everything and withholding their critical judgment. This practice should not remain simply an outer rule of life, but must take hold of the innermost part of the soul. It lies in our hands to perfect ourselves and gradually transform ourselves completely. But this transformation must take place in our innermost depths, in our thinking. Showing respect outwardly in our relations with other beings is not enough; we must carry this respect into our thoughts.

As we contemplate the Foundation Stone Meditation, the Angels, Archangels, and Archai participate with us

Rudolf Steiner, *The First Class Lessons and Mantras,* fifteenth lesson:

At first, we believe that only we experience our thoughts. Yet, all the time that our thoughts pass through our souls the Angeloi are in reality living in them. Just as we sense things with our senses, just as we touch an object and take hold of it, so do the Angeloi live in our thinking. Our thinking is their sensing. They make us aware of this. Just as the Angeloi are sensing in our thinking, so the Archangeloi are experiencing in our feeling, and the Archai are beholding in our willing. My dear sisters and brothers, when any thought passes through your soul, feel that a being of the hierarchy of the Angeloi is sensing something in this thought. Human thinking, human feeling, and human willing are not merely processes inside the human being. While we think, the Angeloi are sensing; when we feel, the Archangeloi are experiencing; and, when we will, the Archai are beholding.

Contemplating the Foundation Stone and being thought by Angels

Rudolf Steiner, *The Fifth Gospel* (CW 148), Lecture of December 18, 1913:

Take a thought, for instance—something that lives in a human mind. Initially thoughts exist in our conscious mind, but not only there. Spirits belonging to the next higher hierarchy, Angeloi or Angels, also have that thought. But whereas we have a single thought, the whole of our thought world is a thought of the Angels. The Angels think our conscious mind. You can see that when you advance in higher vision you need to develop a different feeling for perception of the higher worlds than you do in the world of ordinary physical reality. The mode of thinking we use in relation to the physical world and to existence on Earth will not help us to achieve higher vision. There you need only to think, but also to be thought, and to know that you are being thought.

Angel beings in the gaze of the other

Rudolf Steiner, *The Connection between the Living and the Dead* (CW 168), October 10, 1916:

But when we experience, and as we experience from our imaginations and feelings, the whole world of the hierarchies works into this process. It lives and weaves in it. When you meet a person and look into his eyes, in his look, and in what his look sends to meet you, live the spirits of the hierarchies, live the hierarchies, the work of the hierarchies.

O Man, Know Thyself *sounds from the fixed stars and planets*

Imagine how brilliantly a hundred years ago the starry sky curved over the village of Dornach without any of the current air- and light pollution. For most anthroposophists of the time the stars were familiar friends, they had been brought up with them. They knew the starry constellations and knew the orbits of the planets along the zodiac. They understood from their own experience how attention for the stars and planets leads to the way they become reflected as inner movements in the soul. These days you have to live really far from the city to be able to experience this.

Rudolf Steiner, *The First Class Lessons and Mantras,* eighth lesson:

Today I would like to start—please don't take any notes at this stage; just listen to the words—by speaking the mantric verse that resounds in the human soul, in the heart, as the great challenge to strive for true knowledge of yourself. It has sounded throughout time, first starting in the Mysteries, but the Mysteries received it from the stars, from the writings of the great cosmic script. This challenge rings forth from the entire cosmos: "O Man, Know Thyself!"

If we look up to the fixed stars, to those that stand with a particularly distinct script in the zodiac, which, through their grouping in certain forms (the constellations) bring the great cosmic script to expression, then the content of the Cosmic Word is first revealed to those who understand this script: "O Man, Know Thyself!"

O Man, Know Thyself!
Thus sounds the Cosmic Word.
You hear it with strength of soul,
You feel it with might of spirit.
Who speaks so powerfully through the world?
Who speaks so tenderly within your heart?
Does it work through the far-spread rays of space
Into your senses' experience of life?
Does it sound through the weaving waves of time
Into the evolving stream of your life?
Is it you, yourself, who,
By sensing space, by experiencing time
Begets this word,
Feeling yourself estranged in the psychic void of space,
Because you lose the force of thought
In the annihilating stream of time?

Human soul
you live within the limbs
which bear you through the world of space
into the spirits' ocean-being.

Moral impulses from the Thrones, Cherubim, and Seraphim into our limbs

Rudolf Steiner, *Karmic Relationships, Vol. VII* (CW 239), June 15, 1924:

In the physical human form, the metabolic-limb system is the lowest and therefore has little to do with what is essentially *human* in earthly life, but it is connected in this earthly life with the beings of the highest hierarchy, the Thrones, the Cherubim, and the Seraphim. As we move about the world or work with our hands, in this mysterious activity the activity of the Thrones, Cherubim, and Seraphim is present. These beings remain helpers when man's life continues between death and a new birth. They remain helpers. Now, it is quite erroneous to believe that the moral content of the soul proceeds from the head. In reality, regarded from a higher point of view, man's head is by no means such a tremendously important organ. The head is really more or less a mirror of the external world, and if we had the head alone we should know nothing except the external world. The head simply reflects the external world. The experiences of the head are mirrorings, reflections of the external world. Our inner, moral impulses do not proceed from the head but from the region of the metabolic-limb system, not, however, from the physical system but from its constitution of soul and spirit wherein Thrones, Cherubim, and Seraphim are living.

The human form is the work of Exousiai, Dynameis, Kyriotetes

Rudolf Steiner, *Anthroposophical Leading Thoughts* (CW 26), Michael Letter, page 155:

In these Divine-Spiritual Beings lives the will that man shall be. The will of all these Beings plays a part in the "becoming" of each single human being. The cosmic aim of their harmonious cooperation is the production of the human *form*; for man is still without form in the divine-spiritual world.

It may seem strange that the whole choir of Divine-Spiritual Beings should work for a single human being. But the hierarchies of the Exousiai, Dynameis, Kyriotetes, Thrones, Cherubim, and Seraphim also worked in this way at the still earlier stage throughout the Moon, Sun, and Saturn evolutions, in order that man might come into being.

Our limbs are the integrated thoughts of the Exousiai, Kyriotetes, etc.

"Elohim" is the biblical name of the Creator. According to Rudolf Steiner he belongs to the divine Trinity, and from that sphere he reaches down through the hierarchies into the sphere of the Exousiai, the Spirits of Form, to give human beings their form. The Kyriotetes, or Spirits of Wisdom, think matter, the Dynameis bring matter into movement, the Exousiai create the forms in the sphere of life. We become human beings out of cosmic thoughts.

Rudolf Steiner, *Die Wissenschaft vom Werden des Menschen* (CW 183), August 26, 1918:

What you leave behind in the grave, what is cremated, are merely, I might say, the mineral enclosures. Your arms and hands, your legs and feet are not visible feet, etc.; they are forces, and you take these with you. You take the forms with you. You will say: I have hands and feet. A person who can see into the spiritual world does not say: I have hands and feet. He says: There are Spirits of Form (Elohim, Exousiai) who think cosmically, and their thoughts are my arms and hands, legs and feet; and their thoughts are filled with blood and other saps.

But in turn, blood and other saps are also not that which they physically appear to be; these substances are again the imaginations of the Spirits of Wisdom (Kyriotetes), and what the physicist calls matter is merely external appearance. When the physicist speaks of matter he should really say: I am running into a thought of the Spirits of Wisdom, the Kyriotetes. And when you see arms and hands, legs and feet, you actually cannot come across them, but you would have to say: Here the cosmic thoughts of the Spirits of Form (Exousiai) fashion my forms. In brief, strange as it may sound, your body doesn't exist at all, but there where your body is in space there live the cosmic thoughts of higher hierarchies working together. And if you would not see according to Maya but actual reality, you would say: Even here do the cosmic thoughts of the Exousiai, the Spirits of Form, the Elohim reach. These cosmic thoughts make themselves visible for me since they are filled with the cosmic thoughts of the Spirits of Wisdom (Kyriotetes). This gives us arms and hands, legs and feet. Nothing of what appears through Maya stands before the spiritual gaze; what stands there are cosmic thoughts, and these cosmic thoughts come together, condense, slide into each other, and thus they appear to us as this shadow figure in which we move around, and of which we believe that it is real. The physical human being therefore—it does not exist at all.

The body as the Temple of God

The working of the three hierarchies in the human being and nature

The third hierarchy works in our consciousness.

The second hierarchy works in living nature.

The first hierarchy works in our physical body and in physical nature.

Rudolf Steiner, *Eternal and Transient Elements in Human Life: The Cosmic Past of Humanity and the Mystery of Evil* (CW 184), September 8, 1918:

There is a connection between your astral body and the historical life of humanity. And into the historical life of humanity work the beings of the third hierarchy, who make the historical life of humanity. But when you go further, when you go down to the etheric body, this etheric body turns out to be a very complicated entity. In our current consciousness human beings know little of the entire complexity that underlies this human etheric body. But you get a certain understanding of everything that has to work on this etheric body when you study *An Outline of Esoteric Science*; there you see in the successive Saturn, Sun, and Moon phases the successive incarnations of our earth, how this etheric body is formed out of the whole cosmos, and how the beings of the higher hierarchies work on it. If we put that into a concrete formula, we could from a certain standpoint say: All that which is world becoming, which is now more encompassing, and with which our etheric body is connected just as our astral body is with the historical life of humanity—all this is created and fashioned by the beings of the second hierarchy, the Exousiai, Dynameis, and Kyriotetes.

Therefore, to clarify this I will say: The beings of the second hierarchy make everything that works into the human etheric body. But that brings us to something else. When you wake up in the morning and sink into your etheric body, you actually submerge yourself into the creation of the beings of the second hierarchy. And you also sink into your physical body. What outer anatomy and physiology bring to light of this physical body, which the ancient mysteries correctly called the Temple of God, is really merely the outermost hull. We can only get some idea of this amazing and miraculous structure of the human physical body when we know: it is the creation of the collaboration of the beings of the first hierarchy. When as you wake up in the morning you sink into your physical body, you actually sink into the work of the highest hierarchies.

Think, therefore, of how things in life are arranged. Here between birth and death, when we are awake, we first sink into our astral body, in which the historical life of humanity is active. But we also sink into our etheric body, the creation of the second hierarchy, into which works much from the cosmos, the etheric life of the cosmos. And we sink into our physical body, which is the creation of the beings of the first hierarchy. And when we are living between death and a new birth, we do not live with the creation, but with the Creator himself.

The spiritual hierarchies and their working in space

Rudolf Steiner, *The Fourth Dimension* (CW 324a), Question and answer session April 21, 1909:

Question:
Should we picture the spiritual hierarchies with the concept of space, since we speak of their areas of rulership?

Answer:
Regarding human beings we can say that the spiritual entity of a human being lives within space. From an occult point of view, however, we should imagine space itself also as something that was created. This creation took place before the workings of the highest hierarchies; we should therefore imagine space as previously existing. But we should not picture the highest Trinity as spatial, for space is one of its creations. We should imagine [spiritual] beings as existing without space; space is something that was created. But the workings of the hierarchies in our world are spatially limited, like those of human beings. The other hierarchies move therefore within space.

We are swimming with the head rising a little out of the ocean of the activities of the Hierarchies.

Rudolf Steiner, *Karmic Relationships*, Vol. II (CW 236), May 30, 1924:

And now we have the reason why freedom, free spiritual activity, can be unfolded in earthly life. As long as the Moon was connected with the earth, as long as the primeval teachers taught men out of their store of remembrance, and as long as this teaching was preserved in the Mysteries—actually until the fourteenth century AD—all wisdom consisted in what had been seen with the eye of the gods. Only since the period I indicated to you, only since the year 1413, has it become utterly impossible for the earth to see with the eye of the gods. So that with the development of the consciousness soul, freedom begins to be within the reach of men.

But in point of fact, man is on the earth only in the activity of sense perception and intellectual knowledge, for the latter is also bound up with the physical body. The truth of the matter is as follows. Let us picture the human being. It is only in his sense and intellectual knowledge that he extends beyond the hierarchies, which are within him. In respect of all that lies behind his intellect he is filled with the third hierarchy; in all that lies behind his feeling, he is filled with the second hierarchy; in all that lies behind his willing, he is filled with the first hierarchy.

We are therefore in very truth within the hierarchies and it is only in respect of our sensory organs and intellect that we extend beyond their realm. It is actually as though we were swimming, with our head rising a little out of the water. With our senses and our intellect, we rise out of the ocean of the activities of the hierarchies.

The ether is as an ocean

Rudolf Steiner, *Anthroposophical Leading Thoughts* (CW 26), Letter 24, "Man in His Macrocosmic Nature":

The forces which place the etheric body in the world come from the cosmos *around* the earth; those for the physical body radiate from the *center* of the earth.

But together with the etheric forces which stream to the earth from the sphere of the cosmos there come also the world impulses which work in the astral body of man.

The ether is like an ocean in which the astral forces swim from all directions of the cosmos and approach the earth.

The human being raises himself out of the ocean of spiritual reality

Rudolf Steiner, *Anthroposophical Leading Thoughts* (CW 26), no. 156:

In waking life, to experience *himself* in full and free self-consciousness, man must forego the conscious experience of reality in its true form, both in his existence and in that of nature. Out of the ocean of reality he lifts himself, that in his shadowed thoughts he may make his own I his very own in consciousness.

Practice spirit-recalling
in depths of soul
where in the wielding
World-Creator-Being
your own I
comes into being
in the I of God
and you will truly live
in human world-all being.

First indication of the coming Ex Deo nascimur

Rudolf Steiner gave countless memory exercises, small and more extensive review exercises, review of the day, of recent memories, of our youth, of prior karma, and of world history in the light of the spirit. His book An Outline of Esoteric Science *can also be viewed as a memory exercise at the cosmic level, as a review of the prior incarnations of the earth.*

Rudolf Steiner, *What is Necessary in These Urgent Times* (CW 196), February 13, 1920:

And here I come to an important chapter of spiritual knowledge. Imagine for a moment that in human self-knowledge, you are reflecting on memory, on our ability to recollect. You say: "I am turning my inner organ, my soul organ toward the activity of memory." But when you consider this act from a fully conscious place, then you must also go on to say to yourself: "In this act, in this process of recollection, there are Angels living and moving throughout that inner organ." Take a moment now and try to remember something that you experienced yesterday, some sort of experience that you had. In doing this you have carried out an inner soul process. In the process that occurred, during which a thought from yesterday again appeared within you, an experience of yesterday revealed itself anew in your memory—an Angel is active in all of that activity. And when you think about something intelligently—and it must actually be thinking intelligently, not merely brooding, not merely doing what most people call intelligent thinking, which is really nothing more than cooking one's memory more thoroughly, than allowing the body to stew upon memories. Thinking begins truly when you actively and inwardly take up your thoughts. So, when one develops this sort of inner activity, an Archangel is present for that. And when you so much as listen to or look at what is around you, then you must say to yourself: "In my ears and in my eyes are the thrones of the Archai, the Spirits of Time." When you find yourself asking: "Where are the Spirits of Time, the Archai, who rule over each age of the world as it follows on the next?"—then you should not go looking for them in distant or unfamiliar regions; you need only to look in the sense organs of human beings. That is where they sit. A decadent time (in regard to sense perceptions) has already sought the gods up above in the heavens, where they are not to be found—and the Spirits of Time in the heavens as well, where they are not to be found. When a person asks: "Then where are the Spirits of Time?"—they are sitting in his eyes, in her ears. Their thrones are there.

According to the biblical creation story the "Elohim" were the world creators

Rudolf Steiner, *The Spiritual Hierarchies and the Physical World* (CW 110), question and answer session April 21, 1909:

Question:
Do the Elohim stand even higher than the nine hierarchies?

Answer:
The Elohim are those beings who remained connected with the sun when the sun separated from the earth. They belong to the hierarchy that is called Powers, or Spirits of Form, and to the hierarchies above them. They are still within our development. Elohim is the collective name of the Sun beings. At one time they chose the Sun as their dwelling place, not as their place of influence. Christ, the highest of the Elohim, reigns over them. However, He does not belong to the hierarchies, but to the Trinity. Christ is a being so powerful that it exercises influence on all parts of our solar system.

I am

Rudolf Steiner, *The First Class Lessons and Mantras,* nineteenth lesson:

Whoever wishes to enter the realm of esoteric life should begin by feeling that the sacred, ancient words: "Ejeh Asher Ejeh"—"I am I," "I am"—are indeed the holy words that sound across to us from a reality found on the other side of the threshold. What we take hold of in our fleeting thoughts as "I am" is merely a reflection of the true "I am."

Actually, we must be aware that the true "I am" does not, at first, speak from us within this earthly realm. If we wish to say "I am" truly and worthily, we must first enter the realm of the Seraphim, Cherubim, and Thrones, for only there does the "I am" ring true. Here in the earthly realm it is an illusion.

To experience the true "I am" within us we must hear the Cosmic Word. We must listen to the question the Guardian of the Threshold asks: Who really is speaking in the Cosmic Word? The Seraphim who weave their way through the cosmos with spirit-lightning flames, they speak the fire language of the Cosmic Word, where we now stand. The Word is fire, it is a flaming voice. And to the degree that we experience this burning, cosmic fire that speaks the language of fire with a flaming voice, to that degree do we experience the true "I am."

For the Father-Spirit of the heights holds sway
in depths of worlds begetting life.

The working of the Trinity and the hierarchies in our corporeality

Rudolf Steiner, *Initiation Science and the Development of the Human Mind* (CW 228), September 2, 1923:

Lastly the physical body: if we ourselves had to achieve all the great and wonderful processes taking place there, we should not merely do it very badly; we could not set about it at all. Here we are utterly helpless. What outer anatomy ascribes to the physical body could not even move a single atom of it. Powers of quite another order are required here, namely none other than those that have been known since primeval times as the supreme Trinity—the powers of the Father, Son, and Holy Spirit. They, the essential Trinity, indwell the physical body of man.

Therefore in truth, throughout our earthly life our physical body is not our own. If it depended on us, it could not go on at all. It is, as was said of old, the true Temple of the Godhead, of the divine threefold Being. Likewise, our ether body is the dwelling place of the Seraphim, Cherubim, and Thrones. They have to help in caring for the organs which are assigned to the etheric body. As to those physical and etheric organs, on the other hand, which are deserted every night by the astral body, they are provided for by the second hierarchy, the Kyriotetes, Dynameis, and Exousiai. Lastly, the organs forsaken during sleep by the human ego, have to be cared for in the night by the Angeloi, Archangeloi, and Archai. There is a constant activity within the human being, proceeding not only from man himself. Only in waking life does he live in his bodily nature, so to speak, as a sub-tenant. For at the same time, it is the Temple and the dwelling place of spiritual beings, the beings of the hierarchies.

The highest angelic hierarchy performs the will of the Creator God

Rudolf Steiner, *The Spiritual Hierarchies and the Physical World* (CW 110), April 18, 1909, evening:

Such is the difference between the Seraphim, Cherubim, and Thrones on the one hand, and humanity on the other. From the beginning of their development, these highest beings of the spiritual hierarchies were immediately present with the Godhead, the Divine Trinity. From the very beginning, they enjoyed being within sight of the Divinity. For the Seraphim, Cherubim, and Thrones, the condition that human beings ought to progress toward, existed from the very beginning.

It is extremely important to recognize that, from the time of their origin, these beings beheld God, and that, as long as they live, they will always behold God. They accomplish everything through gazing upon God, and God works through them. They could not do otherwise than act as they do. It would be impossible for them to do otherwise. The sight of God is such a powerful force, has such an influence upon them, that they accomplish what the Godhead ordains with unerring certainty and immediate impulse. Nothing resembling deliberation or judgment exists in the sphere of these beings. There is only the beholding of the Godhead's commands in order to receive the immediate impulse to do what they have beheld. They see the Godhead in its original true form, as it really is. They consider themselves simply as those who fulfill the will and wisdom of the Divine. Such is the situation of the highest hierarchy.

Second indication of the coming Ex Deo nascimur

Rudolf Steiner, *The Mission of the Individual Folk Souls* (CW 121), June 11, 1910:

That which on our earth appears externally for the most part as a fluid element—not the liquid water we see around us today but the primal semi-fluid element which was brought to rest by the Spirits of Form (Exousiai)—this we must look upon as the most external manifestation of the Spirits of Will (Thrones). But another element is always associated with this activity. The Spirits of Will are assisted by the Cherubim or Seraphim. The Cherubim work in the air element, in everything aeriform which permeates the apparent solid substance of the Earth. Air is an illusion behind which stand the mighty beings we call the Cherubim. The Seraphim work in fire, they operate in whatsoever manifests as heat.

Thus we see how the radiations from the center influence our Earth planet. Our planet therefore is so constituted that the Spirits of Will (Thrones), Cherubim, and Seraphim work from the center. We must look upon our planet in this way: at the meeting place of the boundaries of air and heat or warmth—for the atmosphere is just as much part of our planet as the water or dry land—a surface is formed. Upon this surface the Spirits of Form (Exousiai) literally dance upon the waves and bring them to rest and mold them into form. It was for this reason that they were given their name. Behind them are the Spirits of Movement (Dynameis), and in their element again is mingled what we call the Spirits of Wisdom (Kyriotetes). When therefore we look inward toward the center of our planet we are aware of the presence of Divine Beings, Thrones, Cherubim, and Seraphim. When we look outward we perceive first of all beyond the realm of the Spirits of Form, who permeate the air and heat with their element, the Spirits of Movement and the Spirits of Wisdom. When we gaze out into the periphery of the Earth, when we lift our eyes to the Cosmic Spheres, all the nature forces and natural phenomena we encounter there are fundamentally the work of the second hierarchy. Everything we see when we look into the depths of the Earth we ascribe to the beings of the highest hierarchy. It is to the unique cooperative activity of these two hierarchies that we owe the configuration of our environment.

We have stated that the three elements, water, air, and fire are related to the Spirits of Will (Thrones), the Cherubim, and the Seraphim. In which of these elements do the Spirits of Form (Exousiai) manifest themselves? They are the beings nearest to us and they "dance upon" the surface of the Earth where we live and have our being. They work inward from universal space, but now unfold their forces in the emanations issuing from the Earth. To us they are concentrated in the rays of the Sun. Light, therefore, is the element in which the Spirits of Form (Exousiai) first weave and work. Since, however, the activities of light and everything related to it manifest themselves at the frontier where the Spirits of Movement (Dynameis) and Spirits of Will (Thrones) work in concert, it is at this meeting place that solid forms are created.

Seraphim – Cherubim – Thrones
let ring forth from the heights
what in the depths is echoed
speaking
Ex Deo nascimur.

The working of the hierarchies in the physical states of matter

The creative forces of the first and second hierarchy work in matter in its different physical conditions. The second hierarchy works in the movements of water, air, and warmth as the creator of living nature.

Rudolf Steiner, *Genesis: Secrets of Creation* (CW 122), August 22, 1910:

Anyone who wishes to get to the bottom of things has to ask himself which of the hierarchies has brought it about that out of the more rarified warmth substance, the denser air comes into being. It is those very Spirits of Will (Thrones) who sacrificed the warmth substance out of themselves who have brought this about! We may describe their activity by saying that during the Saturn evolution they were so advanced as to be able to allow their own substance to flow out as warmth, so advanced as to be able to offer their own substance as a sacrifice, so advanced that their fire streamed into the planetary existence of Saturn. Then during the Sun evolution they condensed this, their fire, into the gaseous element. But it was also they who during the Moon evolution condensed their gaseous element to water. During the earth evolution they have further condensed their watery element into the earth element, into solid.

[...]

We must not think that we can make a clear separation between these spheres, that we can draw hard and fast boundaries between them. Our entire earth subsists in the fact that watery, aeriform, and solid are working one within another, and that warmth permeates everything. We find warmth everywhere within the other stages of elementary existence. Hence we can also say that we find everywhere the activity of the Elohim (the Creator), the real force behind warmth; it has poured itself out into everything. Although it necessarily required the activities of the Spirits of Will (Thrones), the Spirits of Wisdom (Kyriotetes), the Spirits of Movement (Dynameis), in order to display itself, nevertheless throughout earth evolution this element of warmth, which is the manifestation of the Spirits of Form (Exousiai), permeated all the lower stages of existence. Thus in the solid element we shall find not just the substantial basis, the body of the Spirits of Will, but the body of the Spirits of Will permeated and interwoven by the Elohim themselves, by the Spirits of Form.

[…]

To the seer things are not so simple as that. As soon as things are traced back to their spiritual sources, the same thing is not seen everywhere. Different forces are at work when gas condenses to liquid on earth, and when the gaseous, vaporous tendency in the environment of the earth forms watery cumuli. When the seer contemplates the way in which water arises in the atmosphere around us, he cannot say that it comes into being in the same way as on the ground; he cannot say that the water hovering above us comes into existence in the same way as the water which condenses in the soil, on the ground. For the truth is that the Beings who play their part in cloud formation are different from those who are at work in the formation of water on the earth. What I have just been saying as to the participation of the hierarchies in our elementary existence only applies on the earth from its center point to the surface where we ourselves are; the same forces do not extend as far as the formation of the clouds. There other Beings are at work. The scientific theory derived from modern physics is based on a very simple hypothesis. First it discovers certain physical laws, and then it says that these laws apply to the whole of existence. It overlooks all the differences in the different spheres of existence. It acts on the principle that in the night all cows are grey; but things are not the same everywhere, they are very different in different spheres!

Anyone who has become aware through clairvoyant investigation that on our earth the Spirits of Will (Thrones) hold sway in the earth element, the Spirits of Wisdom (Kyriotetes) in the element of water, the Spirits of Movement (Dynameis) in the aeriform element, the Elohim in the warmth, gradually attains to the knowledge that in the gathering of the clouds, in that unique process which goes on around the earth wherein the watery vapor becomes water, beings belonging to the hierarchy of the Cherubim are at work. Thus in the solid matter of our elementary earth existence, we see a cooperation of the Elohim with the Thrones. In the element of air, in which the Spirits of Movement (Dynameis) hold sway, we see the Cherubim too at work in order that the water mounting upward from the realm of the Spirits of Wisdom (Kyriotetes) may be enabled to accumulate into clouds. In the environment of our earth, the Cherubim hold sway as truly as do the Thrones, the Spirits of Wisdom (Kyriotetes) and the Spirits of Movement (Dynameis) within the elementary existence of our earth.

And now, if we look to the moving being of these cloud formations, we find hidden within them something still deeper, which only occasionally reveals itself—the thunder and lightning which bursts forth from them. This is not something which comes from nowhere. The seer knows that the spirits whom we call the Seraphim move and have their being in this activity.

Within the limits of our earth sphere, if we include the atmosphere around us, we have now found every one of the hierarchical ranks. Thus, in what we experience with our senses we see the manifestation of hierarchical activity. It would be utter nonsense to regard the lightning flashing forth from the cloud as the same thing one sees when one strikes a match. Quite different forces are at work when the element of electricity, which prevails in the lightning, comes forth out of matter. There the Seraphim are at work.

Thus we have rediscovered the totality of the hierarchies in the earth's environment, just as we find them in the cosmos without. The activity of these hierarchies is extended to all that we find in our immediate environment.

Exousiai think our I

Rudolf Steiner quoted the three Rosicrucian sayings in Latin. The first one, Ex Deo nascimur, *literally means:* From God we are born. *The literal translation of the second saying,* In Christo morimur, *is:* In Christ we die. *The third saying,* Per Spiritum Sanctum reviviscimus, *means literally:* Through the Holy Spirit we come back to life. *The sayings were translated by Rudolf Steiner in many variants, often in the first person singular, the form in which the development of the consciousness soul comes to expression. In speaking the threefold sayings in the Foundation Stone Meditation the first, second, and third hierarchies are successively present, while in each panel of the Meditation the meaning of the saying is prepared in the preceding two sentences.*

Rudolf Steiner, *The First Class Lessons and Mantras,* twelfth lesson.

My dear sisters and brothers, in earthly life we think that our thoughts are mere empty nothings. But when a being of the rank of the Exousiai thinks, he thinks in us. *Our* I is being thought. *Our* I exists as a thought of a being of the rank of the Exousiai. If on earth we say to ourselves, what are we beholding? This I, when we speak "I," we look back to this "I" and speak the word I. But for a being of the rank of the Exousiai, the "I" is a thought, a real thought. We *exist* in as much as we are *thought* by beings of the rank of the Exousiai. And when we speak "I" to ourselves, we are actually recognizing that we are thought by divine beings. Our higher self exists because we are being thought by divine beings.

This is heard by the spirits of the elements

in east, west, north, south

may human beings hear it.

A characterization of the elemental beings

Rudolf Steiner, *Spiritual Beings in the Heavenly Bodies and in the Kingdoms of Nature* (CW 136), April 3 and 5, 1912:

This is especially the case if we devote ourselves to the peculiar play of a body of water tossing in a waterfall and giving out clouds of spray, if we yield ourselves to the forming and dissolving mist and to the watery vapor filling the air and rising like smoke, or when we see the fine rain coming down, or feel a slight drizzle in the air. If we feel all this morally there appears a second class of beings, to whom we can apply the word metamorphosis, transformation. As little as we can paint lightning, can we draw this second class of beings. We can only note a shape, present for a moment, and the moment after everything is again changed. Thus there appear to us as the second class of beings, those who are always changing form, for whom we can find an imaginative symbol in the changing formations of clouds.

But as occultists we become acquainted in yet another way with these beings. When we observe the plants as they come forth from the earth in the spring, just when they put forth the first green shoots—not later, when they are getting ready to bear fruit—the occultist perceives that the same beings that he or she discovered in the scattering, drifting, gathering vapors, are surrounding and bathing the beings of the budding plants. So we can say that when we see the plants springing forth from the earth, we see them everywhere bathed by such ever-changing beings as these. Then occult vision feels that what weaves and hovers unseen over the buds of the plants is in some way concerned with what makes the plants push up out of the ground, draw forth from the ground.

You see, ordinary physical science recognizes only the growth of the plants, knows only that the plants have an impelling power that forces them up from below. The occultist, however, recognizes more than this in the case of the blossom. The occultist recognizes—around the young sprouting plant—changing, transforming beings who have, as it were, been released from the surrounding space and penetrate downward; they do not, like the physical principle of growth, merely pass from below upward, but come from above downward, and draw forth the plants from the ground. So in spring, when the earth is robing itself in green, to the occultist it is as though nature forces, descending from the universe, draw forth what is within the earth, so that the inner part of the earth may become visible to the outer surrounding world, to the heavens. Something that is in unceasing motion hovers over the plant. It is characteristic that occult vision acquires a feeling that what floats around the plants is the same as what is present in the rarified water, tossing itself into vapor and rain. That, let us say, is the second class of nature forces and nature beings.

[...]

Just as the plant puts forth seed, so do the beings of the third hierarchy, which I have just described, bring forth other beings. There is, however, a certain difference between what the plant brings forth as seed—if we may use this comparison—and the beings that separate themselves off from the beings of the third hierarchy. When the plant brings forth a seed, it is, in a sense, of as much value as the complete plant; for out of it can arise again a complete plant of the same species. These beings put forth others who are separated from them as the seed is from the plant—they have offspring, so to speak—but the offspring are, in a sense, of a lower order than themselves. They have to be of a lower order because they have other tasks that they can only accomplish if they are of a lower order.

The Angels, Archangels, and Spirits of the Age in our spiritual environment have put forth from themselves certain beings who descend from the human environment into the kingdoms of nature; and occult vision teaches us that the beings we learned about yesterday as the nature spirits are detached from the beings of the third hierarchy we have learned to know today. They are offspring, and to them has been allotted other service to humanity, namely service to nature. Indeed, certain offspring of the Archai are the beings we have learned to know as the nature spirits of the earth; those separated from the Archangels and sent down into nature, are the nature spirits of water; and those separated from the Angels we have recognized as the nature spirits of the air. With the nature spirits of fire or heat we have still to become acquainted.

Thus we see that, in a sense, through a division of the beings who represent, as the third hierarchy, our union with the world immediately above us, certain beings are sent down into the kingdoms of the elements, into air, water, earth—into the gaseous, fluid, and solid—in order to perform service there, to work within the elements, and in a sense to function as the lower offspring of the third hierarchy--as nature spirits. Thus we can speak of a relationship between the nature spirits and the beings of the third hierarchy.

What does technology do to the nature beings?

Rudolf Steiner, *Art as Seen in the Light of Mystery Wisdom* (CW 275), December 28, 1914:

Let us start by looking quite superficially at what happens when we develop modern technology. What is happening in the first place is just work being carried out in two stages. The first stage consists in destroying the interrelationships of nature. We blast out quarries and take the stone away, maltreat the forests and take the wood away, and the list could go on—in short, we get our raw materials in the first instance by smashing and wearing down the interrelationships in nature. And the second stage consists of taking what we have extracted from nature and putting it together again as a machine according to the laws we know as natural laws. These are the two stages, if we look at the matter on the surface.

But what is it like when we look below the surface? Looking at it from inside, the matter is like this. When we take things from nature, mineral nature to begin with, we know from previous lectures that this is linked with a certain feeling of wellbeing belonging to the elemental spiritual beings that are within it. This, however, does not concern us so much now. What is important here is that we cast out of nature the elemental spirits belonging to the sphere of the regular progressive hierarchies who, in fact, are the very spirits who maintain nature. In all natural existence there are elemental spiritual beings. When we plunder nature we squeeze out the nature spirits into the sphere of the spirit. That is, in fact, what is constantly happening during the first stage. We smash and plunder material nature and thus release the nature spirits, driving them forth from the sphere allotted them by the Jehovah gods into a realm where they can fly about freely and are no longer bound to their allotted dwelling places. Thus we can call the first stage the casting out of the nature spirits.

The second stage is the one where we put together what we have plundered from nature, according to our knowledge of natural laws. Now, when we construct a machine or a complex of machines out of raw material according to our knowledge of natural laws, we put certain spiritual beings into the things we construct. The structure we make is by no means without its spiritual beings. In constructing it we make a habitation for other spiritual beings, but these spiritual beings that we conjure into our machines are beings belonging to the ahrimanic hierarchy. Thus at the first stage we encounter nature beings who are in progressive evolution and cast them out; at the second stage we unite these ahrimanic spirits with our mechanisms or other products of technology.

Laying a foundation stone in 1909

The spirits of the four winds had been evoked earlier by Rudolf Steiner in a slightly different form, at the inauguration of the Dome of Malsch in 1909.

Rudolf Steiner, *Rosicrucianism Renewed* (CW 284), April 6, 1909:

We want to call down upon this stone and the Malsch Lodge the blessing of the Masters of Wisdom and Harmony of Feelings and the blessing of all the high and highest beings, the spiritual hierarchies, who are connected with earth evolution. We implore that they let their power stream into this foundation stone and allow it to work on within it so that all that is thought, felt, willed, and done over this stone may be in harmony with them and be ensouled by their spirit.

> Let the light of the Spirits of the East
> Shine upon this building;
> May the Spirits of the West let it ray back;
> May the Spirits of the North strengthen it
> And the Spirits of the South warm it through,
> So that the spirits of the East, West, North, and South
> Stream through the building.

Contemplations for the Second Panel

Human soul
you live within the beat of heart and lung
which leads you through the rhythms of time
into the feeling of your own soul-being.

The movements of the planets and the beat of heart and lung

Rudolf Steiner, *The First Class Lessons and Mantras,* eleventh lesson:

If we enter meditatively into our breast, we feel movement. This movement is an image of the movement of the planets, of the sun, the moon, Mars, Mercury, Jupiter, Venus, and Saturn. The Sun, which feels closest to us, represents this movement. With its apparent course around the Earth each day, the Sun may stand as a representative. Just as we carry the star-filled places of the world, the homeland of the gods, rolled up inside our head, so do we carry the movement of the entire planetary system—represented by the Sun—in our breathing, in our blood circulation, and in all that is in movement in our organism.

Therefore, we must imagine that just as the majesty of the dwelling places of the gods was first announced like a trumpet call from all sides of the world, so now all that the movements of the planets, represented by the Sun, say to us will flow through our body like a melodious sound.

The stars and planets in the soul

Rudolf Steiner, *The First Class Lessons and Mantras,* ninth lesson:

By "inward" is meant that we have looked at the stars ever so often and have kept a picture of this vision in our soul. Then we no longer depend upon seeing the external starry sky in order to activate in our consciousness the majestic image of the vault of heaven, with the stars shining down upon us. When this image arises from our own inner activity, if the soul has the power to create this image by itself, then the soul will first be able to free itself from the body through its strengthened forces.

In our respiration the spirits of the winds play with us, and we join them

Rudolf Steiner, *The First Class Lessons and Mantras,* fifth lesson:

Air is outside of us. The same air that is outside us is inside us a moment later, and then is outside us again. But we aren't aware of this. Just as we carry our muscles and bones inside us, but only become conscious of their origins in embryonic life and their demise in death, so we are barely aware that we always carry an air-being within us. We continually carry air within us, releasing it and receiving it back again, so that we become one with the entire weaving, living being of the air element where we, as terrestrial creatures, live our lives.

This is no longer the case the minute we enter spiritual realms. At that moment we begin to feel how with every exhalation, with every breathing out, we fly out on the wings of the exhaled air into the wide expanses of existence where the exhaled air disperses. And we feel how by breathing in we take into us the spiritual beings who live in the circulating air. The spiritual world flows into us when inhaling; our own being goes out into the environment when exhaling.

Archangeloi and Angeloi in the fifth post-Atlantean epoch

Rudolf Steiner, *The Fall of the Spirits of Darkness* (CW 177), October 28, 1917:

All things physical are in the image of the spirit. Looking for the indirect route by which the Archangels guided humanity by working with the Angels during the fourth post-Atlantean age, we can say: This was done via the human blood. And the social structure was also created via the blood, for it was based on blood relationship, on blood bonds. Both the Archangels and the Angels had their dwelling place in the blood, as it were. Truly, the blood is not merely something for chemists to analyze; it is also the dwelling place of entities from higher worlds.

During the fourth post-Atlantean age, therefore, the blood was the dwelling place of Archangels and Angels. This is changing with the fifth post-Atlantean age, for the Angels—I am referring to the Angels of Light, the normal Angels—will take possession more of the blood, and the Archangels will be more involved in the nervous system.

Practice spirit-sensing
in balance of the soul
where the surging deeds
of world-evolving
unite
your own I
with the I of the world
and you will truly feel
in human soul's creating.

Balance of soul as the mission of the Earth

Rudolf Steiner, *The Mission of the Individual Folk Souls* (CW 121), June 11, 1910:

What, then, is the mission of the Spirits of Form? What is the real mission of the Earth? If one associates the Old Saturn mission with the endowment of the element of will, the Old Sun mission principally with the endowment of the element of feeling, and the Moon mission chiefly with that of the element of thought—with the human astral body—then the mission of the Earth is to bring about a perfect harmony between these three elements, each of which had been predominant in an earlier incarnation of our Earth. The mission of our Earth is to resolve the conflict between these elements and restore a proper harmony between them.

Human beings are involved in this mission of the Earth in order that they may establish this harmony between thinking, feeling, and willing, first of all in their own inner being. At the beginning of the Earth period human beings were in this respect a patchwork of thought, feeling, and will. Everyone who possesses a little self-knowledge can feel that humanity of today has not yet achieved inner harmony; they are frequently victims of conflict and discord. Humanity is called upon, first of all, to strike a balance between thought, feeling, and will within themselves by means of which they themselves as Ego-beings can demonstrate and communicate to their fellow men what this harmony signifies.

About world-evolving deeds

Rudolf Steiner, *The First Class Lessons and Mantras,* tenth lesson:

Yes, my dear friends, my sisters and brothers, the zodiac speaks a significant language when we no longer look at it from the perspective of the Earth—Ram, Bull, Twins, Crab, Lion, etc. It speaks a different language when we circle around it from the other side. This is a deed from our consciousness; we begin to read the secrets of worlds. We read the deeds of spiritual beings [...] We read the spiritual deeds of spiritual beings who have brought everything into existence.

Stars, Soul, and World

Rudolf Steiner, *The First Class Lessons and Mantras,* tenth lesson:

We can look up to the planets, we look at the stars and fill ourselves with the endless majesty of what comes toward us from the universe. We then say to ourselves: We are as connected to what shines down upon us from the cosmos as we are connected to all that surrounds us in our physical environment.

Feeling in love for the wandering stars or planets

Rudolf Steiner, *The First Class Lessons and Mantras,* ninth lesson:

Because we feel love in our soul for the movement of the planets (meaning we feel love for the spiritual beings who live there), we experience the powers orbiting in cosmic space as feeling. If we are able to say: The Sun moves in cosmic space as feeling; Mercury moves in cosmic space as feeling; Mars moves in cosmic space as feeling; then we have grasped feeling in its cosmic essence when it is separated from thinking and willing.

Exousiai, Dynameis, Kyriotetes weaving in our etheric body

Rudolf Steiner, *Die menschliche Seele in ihrem Zusammenhang mit göttlich-geistigen Individualitäten* (CW 224), May 2, 1923:

Now only have you extracted from the word *etheric body* what the real etheric body of the human being actually is. It is the working together, flowing together, weaving together of the Exousiai, Dynameis, Kyriotetes, who individualize their streaming, flowing, sounding, speaking activities and fashion the human etheric body. But when we observe that which, individualizing, the Kyriotetes, Dynameis, and Exousiai fashion in such a way that, shining in its individualizing, warming, sounding, speaking fashions the human physical body, then we have also arrived at the astral body of the human being. For this moving action, this individualizing activity of the second hierarchy that streams from the cosmos but is individualized in the human being, encompasses that which is the human astral body. This activity shows itself in the etheric body; in the astral body it *is*.

For the Christ-will encircling us holds sway

in world rhythms, bestowing grace upon souls.

Streams of spiritual beings from three spheres, when we fall asleep

We move outside our skin up to the sphere of the Angels, Archangels, and Archai, the third hierarchy. We see how the daily movement of the sun from sunrise to sunset directs life processes in nature, a working of the second hierarchy.

But we also see how the sun moves slowly, every day one degree against its daily movement, through the whole zodiac, so that from its lowest point in winter it reaches its highest point in summer in half a year, with all its consequences for our physical circumstances, cold and warmth, humidity and drought—workings of the first hierarchy.

From a Copernican point of view, the East-West movement does not count because it depends on the rotation of the earth and brings us sunrise, the apogee of the sun, and sunset.

But the West-East movement is, when viewed from the earth and also when viewed in the Copernican system from the sun, a West-East movement, for it is dependent on the orbit of the earth around the sun. In this regard, therefore, one can say: the Copernican system relates only to the first hierarchy, not to the second and the third.

Rudolf Steiner, *The First Class Lessons and Mantras,* fifteenth lesson:

This is the skin of our body (a white line is drawn); the more we go out, the more we come from the regions of the Angeloi into those of the Archangeloi and Archai in a radial direction. Thus we come into the third hierarchy. And when we there, falling asleep with our memories and gestures, submerge as in the flowing sea of the weaving entities of the Angeloi, Archangeloi, and Archai, when we dive into this, then comes from one side a stream of spiritual beings (see drawing). This is the second hierarchy, the Exousiai, Dynameis, Kyriotetes. And when we want to bring this into agreement with what is in the outer world, then this stream follows the course in which the second hierarchy crosses the third, the direction that is given to us by the course of the sun, from east to west. The third hierarchy, the Angeloi, Archangeloi, and Archai, float up and down, as it were, and floating up and down they extend the "golden buckets" (Goethe's *Faust*) to each other.

In this picture the second hierarchy goes with the Sun from East to West, in this case not apparently because the Copernican world view does not apply to it, but it is indeed the stream from East to West which the Sun goes through during the day. As human beings behold this—that is, if they are able to behold it—they grow into this third hierarchy during sleep. But this third hierarchy is always mercifully filled from the side by the second hierarchy. And this second hierarchy always comes into play in our soul life.

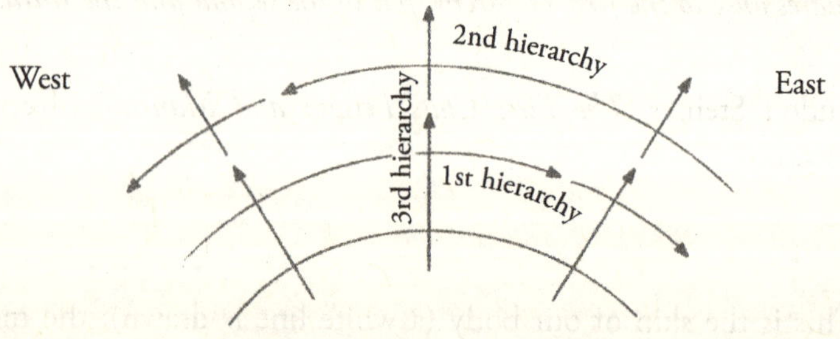

Now, the length of the day varies throughout the year. In spring it lengthens, in the fall it shortens, in summer it is at its longest, in winter at its shortest. The day goes through metamorphoses during the year. This comes from a stream that moves opposite to the East-West stream and goes from West to East (with the movement of the sun through the zodiac). This is the stream of the first hierarchy, the Seraphim, Cherubim, and Thrones. If you, therefore, follow how the day changes in the course of the year, if you proceed from the day to the year, you end up in that which meets you during sleep as the opposite stream

Kyriotetes – Dynameis – Exousiai

let from the east be enkindled

what through the west takes on form

and speaks

In Christo morimur.

Christ holds sway through the second hierarchy

Christ holds sway in all rhythms, of the sun, the moon, and the other planets, in all rhythms and movements on earth, in day and night, in the seasons, in the tides, in storms, wind and weather, in the movements of animals and humans, in our heart-lung rhythm, and in the movements of our soul.

Rudolf Steiner, *The Festivals and their Meaning* (CW 236), June 4, 1924:

On Christmas night, human beings, as they stand here upon the earth with their physical, etheric, and astral bodies, feel themselves related to the threefold cosmos, which appears to them in its etheric nature, shining so majestically, and with the magic wonder of the night in the blue of the heavens; while face to face with them is the astral of the universe, in the stars that glitter in toward the earth. As they realize how the holiness of this cosmic environment is related to what is on the earth itself, they feel that they themselves with their own ego have been transplanted from the cosmos into this world of space. And now they may gaze upon the Christmas mystery—the newborn child, the Representative of Humanity on earth who, inasmuch as he is entering into childhood, is born into this world of space. In the fullness and majesty of this Christmas thought, as they gaze upon the child that is born on Christmas night, they exclaim: "*Ex Deo nascimur*—I am born out of the Divine; the Divine weaves and surges through the world of space."

When we have felt this, when we have permeated ourselves through and through with it, then we may also recall what anthroposophy has revealed to us about the meaning of the earth. The child on whom we are gazing is the outer sheath of that which is now born into space. But whence is he born, that he might be brought to birth in the world of space? According to what we have explained today, it can only be from time. From out of time the child is born.

If we then follow out the life of this child and his permeation by the Spirit of the Christ Being, we come to realize that this being, this Christ Being, comes from the sun. Then we shall look up to the sun, and say to ourselves: "As I look up to the sun, I must behold in the sunshine that time, which in the world of space is hidden. Within the sun is time, and from out of the time that weaves and works within the sun, Christ came forth, came out into space, onto the earth."

And what have we then in Christ on earth? In Christ on earth we have that, which coming from beyond space, from outside of space, unites with the earth.

I want you to realize how our conception of the universe changes, in comparison with the ordinary present-day conception, when we really enter into all that has come before our souls this evening. There in the universe we have the sun, with all that there appears to us to be immediately connected with it—all that is contained in the blue of the heavens, in the world of the stars. At another point of the universe we have the earth with humanity. When we look up from the earth to the sun, we are at the same time looking into the *flow of time*.

Now from this there follows something of great significance. Man only looks up to the sun in the right way (even if it be put in his mind) when, as he gazes upward, he forgets space and considers time alone. For in truth, the sun does not only radiate light, it radiates space itself, and when we are looking into the sun we are looking out of space into the world of time. The sun is the unique star that it is because when we gaze into the sun, *we are looking out of space*. And from that world, outside of space, Christ came to humanity. At the time when Christianity was founded by Christ on earth, humanity had been all too long restricted to the mere *Ex Deo nascimur*, they had become altogether bound up in it, they had become space beings pure and simple.

The reason why it is so hard for us to understand the traditions of primeval epochs, when we go back to them with the consciousness of present-day civilization, is that they always had in mind time, and not the world of space. They regarded the world of space only as an appendage of the world of time.

Christ came to bring the element of time again to humanity, and when the human heart, the human soul, the human spirit unite themselves with Christ, then humanity receives once more the stream of time that flows from eternity to eternity. What else can we human beings do when we die, i.e. when we go out of the world of space, than hold fast to Him who gives time back to us again? At the Mystery of Golgotha, humanity had become beings of space to such an extent that time was lost to them. Christ brought time back again to humanity.

If then, in going forth from the world of space, we would not die in our souls as well as in our bodies, we must die in Christ. We can still be human beings of space and say: *Ex Deo nascimur*, and we can look to the child who comes forth from time into space, that he may unite Christ with humanity. But since the Mystery of Golgotha we cannot conceive of death, the bound of our earthly life, without this thought: "We must die in Christ." Otherwise we shall pay for our loss of time with the loss of Christ Himself and, banished from Him, remain held spellbound. We must fill ourselves with the Mystery of Golgotha. In addition to the *Ex Deo nascimur*, we must find the *In Christo morimur*. We must bring forth the Easter thought in addition to the Christmas thought. Thus the *Ex Deo nascimur* lets the Christmas thought appear before our souls, and the *In Christo morimur* the Easter thought.

[...]

Let us now imagine first of all the inner mood of our soul to be such that we shut ourselves up entirely within this earth existence. We can still feel the Divine, for out of the Divine we are born: *Ex Deo nascimur.* Then let us imagine that we are no longer shutting ourselves up within the mere world of space, but are receiving the Christ who came from the world of time into the world of space, who brought time itself into earthly space. If we do this, then in death we will overcome death. *Ex Deo nascimur. In Christo morimur.*

But Christ Himself brings the message that when space is overcome and one has learned to recognize the sun as the creator of space, when one feels oneself transplanted through Christ into the sun, into the living sun, then the earthly physical vanishes and only the etheric and the astral are there. Now the etheric comes to life, not as the blue of the sky, but as the lilac-red gleaming radiance of the cosmos, and forth from the reddish light the stars no longer twinkle down upon us but gently touch us with their loving effluence.

If we really enter into all this, we can have the experience of ourselves, standing here upon the earth, the physical put aside, but the etheric still with us, streaming through and out of us in the lilac-reddish light. No longer now are the stars glimmering points of light; they are radiations of love like the caressing hand of a human being. As we feel all this—the divine within ourselves, the divine cosmic fire flaming forth from within us as the very being of man; ourselves within the etheric world and experiencing the living expression of the spirit in the astral cosmic radiance—there bursts forth within us the inner awakening of the creative radiance of the spirit, which is man's high calling in the universe.

When those to whom Christ revealed these things had let the revelation sink deep into their being, then the moment came when they experienced the working of this mighty concept, in the fiery tongues of Pentecost. At first they felt the falling away, the discarding of the earthly-physical as death. But then the feeling came: This is not death, but in the place of the physical of the earth there now dawns upon us the spirit-selfhood of the universe—*Per Spiritum Sanctum reviviscimus.*

Thus we may regard the threefold nature of the one half of the year. We have the Christmas thought—*Ex Deo nascimur*; the Easter thought—*In Christo morimur*; and the Whitsun thought—*Per Spiritum Sanctum reviviscimus.*

The Father can be found in outer reality
The Son in the soul
The Spirit in inner reality

Rudolf Steiner, *Building Stones for an Understanding of the Mystery of Golgotha* (CW 175), April 10, 1917:

There is something here that must be clearly understood. For if one follows the path of outward observation to its logical conclusion by studying the physical organism, one arrives at the idea of a universal divinity, an idea which represents the limit of the knowledge of the mysticism—and the associated philosophy—to which I referred at the beginning of this lecture. If, however, one wants to study the soul, one needs to follow the path to that Being whom we call the Christ, who is not to be found in nature, although He has a relationship to it; rather He must be found in history as a historical being. A path of self-observation is related to the spirit and to its repeated earthly incarnations.

A study of the cosmos and of nature leads to the universal divinity that underlies the process of our birth: *Ex Deo nascimur.*

A study of a true historical record leads to a knowledge of Christ Jesus, provided that it can be pursued sufficiently far—to the knowledge that we need if we want to know about the destiny of the soul: *In Christo morimur.*

Inward contemplation, spiritual experience, leads to a knowledge of the spirit in repeated earthly lives and—provided that a connection is found with the spiritual environment in which it dwells—leads to an intuitive knowledge of the Holy Spirit: *Per Spiritum Sanctum reviviscimus.*

Two worldviews, two dangers

Rudolf Steiner, *The Mystery of Death* (CW 159), May 15, 1915:

This is one danger, to tear the roses from the cross and to have only the black, charred cross. The other danger is to tear the cross from the roses and to want to aspire only to the spirit, to despise that which the Godhead itself has placed within world evolution, not to want lovingly to embrace the thought that what is here in the sense world is an expression of the divinity. This is the one-sided religious view of the world which despises science, which wants only the roses and unconsciously aspires toward the luciferic element of the East—just as the science that wants to tear the roses from the cross and wants merely to retain the charred cross aspires toward the West. But we in Central Europe are called upon to have the roses on the cross, to have what is expressed only through the connection of the roses with the cross. And as we look upon the bare, inflexible cross we feel that what has come into the world as rigid matter has come into the world through the Gods. It is as if the spiritual world has created for itself a circle within the material world. *Ex Deo nascimur.*

We feel, too, that—if we understand it rightly—we should not merely enter with Lucifer into the spiritual world but that we die, in that we are connected with what has come down into the world from the divine higher Self: *In Christo morimur.*

And in combining the cross with the roses, the material world conception with the spiritual world conception, we feel how the soul of man can awaken in the Spirit: *Per Spiritum Sanctum reviviscimus.*

This is heard by the spirits of the elements

in east, west, north, south

may human beings hear it.

A character sketch of the elemental beings

Rudolf Steiner, *Harmony of the Creative Word: The Human Being and the Elemental, Animal, Plant and Mineral Kingdoms* (CW 230), November 4, 1923:

Just as we come to know the beings in the sensory world only by observing them in their lives and doings, this is also true in the case of those beings of which I have spoken to you in these lectures, the elemental beings in nature that live behind the sensory-physical and are also involved in everything that happens in the world, or are actually involved in a higher sense than the sensory beings. Now, you can imagine that the world looks different to these beings than to the beings of the sensory world, for you have already seen that these beings do not have a physical body such as the beings of the sensory world. Everything they perceive, observe in the world has to be different from that which penetrates into the human eye. And that is indeed the way it is. For example, human beings experience the earth as the world body on which they move. They experience it even as a slight inconvenience when this world body, as happens now and then, is a little weakened because of particular events in the atmosphere and they sink into it a little bit. They would like to experience this earth ground as hard, as something they do not sink down into.

This experience, this whole attitude toward the earth, is something we will, for example, not find at all with the gnomes; they sink down everywhere, because for them the whole earth body is like a completely hollow space. They can get into it everywhere; for them stone or metal are not things that hinder them from wandering right through it—yes, should I say swim around in it? Our language lacks words to express the movements of these gnomes in the body of the earth—only to say that they have an inner feeling, an inner experience from the different ingredients of the earth. They feel differently when they wander along a metallic deposit than when they go by a layer of limestone. The gnomes feel this inwardly; they penetrate into all these things. They actually have no idea that there is an earth; they have the picture that there is a space in which they have different experiences: gold experiences, mercury experiences, tin experiences, silica experiences, etc. This is here expressed in human language, not in the language of the gnomes, which is much more picture-like. They become that way because their whole life long they run down all the veins, all the layers again and again, and develop this highly developed intellectuality I have mentioned before. In this way they develop their encompassing knowledge, because everything that exists in the world-all outside reveals itself in the metals and in the earth. As in a mirror they experience everything that exists out there in the world-all.

But the earth itself, the gnomes never even notice it, only its different ingredients, the different kinds of inner experience. But these gnomes are extremely gifted observers of the impressions that come from the moon. They continually observe the moon with the greatest attention. In this regard—I can't say born neurasthenics—they became neurasthenics, so to say. True, what for us is an illness is for these gnome beings actually their life element. For them it is no illness, for them it is something obvious. It gives them the receptivity for everything I have mentioned to you. But it gives them also the inner receptivity for the changing phases of the moon. They follow the phases of the moon with such attention that it even changes their form. As a result, when one follows gnome existence, one has a completely different impression at the time of the full moon, new moon, and the phases in between. At full moon the gnomes feel uncomfortable; they don't like the physical moon light and therefore they push their whole feeling of existence outside. When it is full moon they clothe themselves, so to say in a spiritual skin; they push their feeling of existence to the outside of their bodies. And at full moon they appear, when one is able to behold such things imaginatively, I would say, as radiating, armored little knights. Then they are wearing something like a spiritual armor around them, and that is what in their skin pushes its way out, to keep the moonlight away, which is unpleasant for them.

But when the moon approaches new moon, the gnomes become downright transparent, wonderful; one can see a shining, glittering play of colors in them. One sees how a whole world happens in them. It is as if one, I would say, looked into the human brain, but not just like a scientist who is looking for cell tissue, but like someone who is seeing the thoughts shine and sparkle. Thus these gnomes appear to us like transparent little men in whose inner being the whole play of thoughts becomes visible. They are especially interesting at new moon, because each of them bears a whole world in himself, and one can say: In this inner world rests actually the secret of the moon.

If we reveal this moon secret we arrive at most remarkable results; we then discover that the moon these days is coming closer all the time. Of course, you should not imagine this in any crude way, as if it was rushing to the earth, but every year it is coming a little bit closer. And actually, every year the moon is a little closer to the earth. We notice that in the ever more lively play of the moon forces in the world of the gnomes at new moon. And these pixies keep a close eye on this movement of the moon to the earth, because to develop results from what the moon does to them—that is actually their big mission in the world-all. Under great stress they await the moment when the moon will unite again with the earth, and they gather all their forces to be ready for this time when the moon has united again with the earth. For then they will use the moon substance to scatter the substance of the earth gradually into the world-all. The substance has to disappear.

But because they have taken on this task, these kobolds, these gnomes feel very important, for they have the most varied experiences in the whole of earth existence, and they prepare for the time when the entire substance of the earth has been scattered in the world-all and Jupiter is developing, to preserve in the structure of the earth what is good in that structure, and incorporate this like a kind of skeleton into Jupiter.

You see, when we look at all this about the gnomes we first get the impulse to imagine—and we can indeed do this—what our earth would look like if we would take all water away from it. Just think of how on the western hemisphere everything is oriented North-South, and on the eastern hemisphere East-West. Therefore, if you would do away with water, you would see America, with its mountains and with that which is under the sea, become like something that develops from North to South. And looking at Europe, you would see what is in the East-West direction of the Alps and Carpathian Mountains. You would arrive at something like the structure of the cross in the earth. And when we penetrate into this, we receive the impression that it is actually the united gnome world of Old Moon. Those who are the forbears of our earth gnomes, the moon gnomes, have collected their moon experiences and have built this firm structure, this firm structure of the earth body, out of their experience, so that we actually owe our firm earth body to the experiences of the Old Moon gnomes.

These are things we become aware of with regard to the gnome world. They show the gnomes in an extraordinarily interesting relation to the whole evolution of the world-all. In a way they always bring the solid from the past into the solid of the future. They preserve the continuity of the solid structure in evolution. Thus they preserve solid structure from one world incarnation to the next. It is one of the most interesting things to approach these spiritual beings in the spiritual world and to study their particular task. For only in that way does one get the impression how all the beings in the world work together on the entire creation of the world.

Continued with the Contemplations for the third panel.

Contemplations for the Third Panel

Human soul
you live within the resting head
which from the grounds of eternity
unlocks for you world-thoughts.

The human head and the divine hierarchies

Rudolf Steiner, *The Connection between the Living and the Dead* (CW 168), February 22, 1916:

The human head is such a sublime image or copy of the universe in its structure that human beings themselves cannot construct it; even with our life's wisdom woven into us, we could not prepare it for the next incarnation. All of the hierarchies of the gods must play a part in it. What is present in your head, in this sphere, broken only by the occiput—this somewhat transformed sphere—is a real microcosm, a real impression of the great world globe. Everything that lives outside in the universe lives within it; everything that is active in the various hierarchies works there. While we construct our next incarnation from the wisdom collected as a result of our becoming tired as we age, all the hierarchies influence this activity in order to incorporate into us what then becomes the head as an impression of all the wisdom of the gods.

Thinking and will

Rudolf Steiner, *The First Class Lessons and Mantras,* seventh lesson:

In the sense world we think that our thoughts—our mental images—live inside our head. So it is... for the sense world. Nevertheless, a little bit of will is always mixed in with the thinking of the head. This is perceptible even to ordinary consciousness, for when we move from one thought to another we must exert as much will as when we move an arm or a leg, or want anything. Yet it is a very gentle and refined will that leads one thought into the next. That's the way it is in the world of the senses: a wide range of thinking and a little will, a touch of will, are connected with the head. But as soon as we cross the threshold and approach the Guardian the opposite is true: only a little thinking and a vast amount of will are connected with the head. And in this will, which is otherwise asleep in us, we feel the spirit working from the cosmos, working from the heavens, and forming the human head into a spherical image of itself in every detail.

Thinking is light

Rudolf Steiner, *The First Class Lessons and Mantras,* fifth lesson:

And now we approach "light," the light in which we move and live. Except that we don't notice light because with our everyday, normal consciousness we have no idea that the inner weaving of light is contained in our thinking. We have no idea that every thought is "captured light"—both for those with sight and those who are blind. Light is something objective. Not only those who can see light receive light, but also the physically blind receive light when they are thinking. The thoughts we hold fast within us, the thoughts we inwardly capture, are present within us as light.

Battle between light and darkness

Rudolf Steiner, *The First Class Lessons and Mantras,* fifth lesson:

We must become aware of how we are related to light and how light becomes related to us in our esoteric experience of the world. But then, the moment you step over the threshold, it becomes clear that light assumes a quality of being, it becomes *being*, it has to wage a hard battle with the forces of darkness. Something now occurs to a person so that they say to themselves: "If I merge my thinking completely with light, I will lose myself in the light." The minute I merge my thinking with light, then light beings take hold of me and say: "You, human, we will not release you from the light again. We will keep you in the light." This expresses the will of the light beings. They want to draw human beings to them forever through their human thinking. They want to make them one with the light; they want to tear human beings away from all earthly powers and weave them into the light. Beings of light are all around us who, in every moment of our lives, would like to tear us away from the earth and weave us into the sunlight that sweeps over the Earth. These light beings, who live in the surroundings of the Earth, say to us: "You humans should not remain with your soul in your body. With the first rays of the morning sun you should shine down upon the Earth itself, and should set with the evening red of sunset. You should encircle the Earth as Light!"

[...]

As we swing from light into darkness we fall in the opposite extreme. So, this Self who wanted to surge into the bright, shining sunlight is now threatened in the darkness by loneliness, by being separated from all other beings. We human beings can only live in the zone of equilibrium between light and darkness.

The starry world as germ of our thinking

Rudolf Steiner, *The First Class Lessons and Mantras,* eleventh lesson:

The stars are above us and their shining rays come toward us when we look up to them. But they do not only approach us, we also receive them. And we enclose what we receive from the stars within our head. From this sprouts and grows the most human activity on Earth: our thinking.

Practice spirit-beholding
in stillness of thought
where the gods' eternal aims
bestow
the light of cosmic being
on your own I
for free and active willing
and you will truly think
in human spirit depths.

Spirit beholding

Rudolf Steiner, *Sexuality, Inner Development, and Community Life: Ethical and Spiritual Dimensions of the Crisis in the Anthroposophical Society in Dornach, 1915* (CW 253), September 12 and 14, 1915:

Thus, if we really want to enter the spiritual world, we must try to identify our own self with the things around us in such a way that we become accustomed to breaking free of ourselves as we look at higher worlds. I have described this in the last chapter of *Theosophy*; basically, all the indications are already given there. If we become accustomed to doing this, we will gradually begin to experience things in the other way I described. This is not something we can accomplish purely through our own efforts; all we can do is set out on the right path. The experience of being perceived by spiritual beings of the higher hierarchies comes to us as an act of grace on the part of the spiritual world itself. And it is not simply that higher beings look at us; we become perceptions, concepts, and thoughts for the beings of the higher worlds in the same way that objects on the physical plane are for us.

[...]

After that, however, there is still one more thing we must accomplish. When we have really reached the stage of thinking in pure thoughts, when a sequence of pure thoughts is present in our soul, then our personal mind or subjective I is no longer involved. This accounts for the severity we experience when we reach this stage of pure thinking. It is no longer possible to bend things to fit into the mold of how we subjectively would like to have them. Take a train of thought like that of *The Philosophy of Freedom*. It is impossible to construct it in any other way. It cannot be arbitrarily tampered with; you have to let it grow inside you like a living organism. Then your I is really uninvolved; it is thinking itself that is doing the thinking.

Thinking-feeling-will in their mutual dynamics

Rudolf Steiner, *The First Class Lessons and Mantras,* ninth lesson:

Bring into your thinking
Feeling and will
That irradiate the light-filled soul
As pure reflection.
And you are a spirit
Among pure spirits.

Bring into your feelings
Thinking and will
That weave throughout the soul
With warmth as noble love.
And you are a soul
In the realm of the spirits.

Bring into your powers of will
Thinking and feeling
That actively live in your soul
As spirit impulse.
And you see yourself
As a body from spiritual heights.

Angels are thought-beings, but also more than thought-beings

The word substance *ended up in the Latin tradition as the translation of the Greek word* ousia. Ousia *is the noun of the verb* to be. *It means that which is, "being," something that has the quality of being, a gift of the "being-awakening" Father Spirit, which is called* Elohim *in the Bible and works down into all the hierarchies.* Ousia *is what a thing or a being wants to be; a little sunflower wants to become a big sunflower. A good plan has "substance" if it contains unity, form, and will power. Then it has* ousia *and can become something.*

Rudolf Steiner, *Inner Reading and Inner Hearing: How to Achieve Existence in the World of Ideas* (CW 156), December 19, 1914:

When we consider the sleeping human being again we may say: Inasmuch as this sleeping person is outside his physical and etheric bodies, he lives in the world of living thoughts into which the beings of the higher hierarchies are interwoven. But there is also something else that permeates and streams through this world. What is this? The beings of the higher hierarchies are not merely thought beings, they are real beings, they have substance. And that which they have as their substance, we do not experience this in our thoughts, but in our will, namely in the will filled with love. When we bring down moral impulses into our will, which is otherwise only an image for us, we pull the substance of higher beings down into our world. What we really do out of moral impulses is none other than bringing the substance of the beings of the higher hierarchies down into our world.

The consciousness soul begins to develop in the fourth century

Rudolf Steiner, *The Driving Force of Spiritual Powers in World History* (CW 222), March 17, 1923:

Before the fourth Christian century the Spirits of Form held sway, not only in the impressions of the sense world, but above all, also in the thoughts. The thoughts now pass over to the Archai. These beings are, however, nearer to humanity than the Spirits of Form [Exousiai], for their realm lies between humanity and the world of the senses; only, because they are by nature supersensible, humanity is not aware of them. Then come the Archangeloi, then the Angeloi, then humanity itself, and then the animals, plants, and minerals.

So during the period I have indicated, this great, all-embracing, mighty deed lies behind the scenes of world history: the thoughts which are in the things and which human beings draw out of the things, are no longer solely the possession of the Exousiai, the Elohim, but of the Archai.

We "crawl" into the inner being of the Angels, Archangels, Archai

Rudolf Steiner, *Kunst- und Lebensfragen im Lichte der Geisteswissenschaft* [Questions of art and life in the light of spiritual science] (CW 162), July 17, 1915:

Speaking from the viewpoint of the other creatures on the earth we might say: the beings of the different kingdoms, the plant, animal, and mineral kingdoms, allow us to observe them; they are observed by us. Now, it is only a little step for human beings to apply what they have become so used to viewing as their relationship to the world also in the case of beings of a higher order, such as the beings of the higher hierarchies. Human beings imagine that when they ascend into the higher worlds the Angels, Archangels, Spirits of Personality, etc. will be spread around them just as the minerals, plants, and animals are spread around them on the earth. I have to say: It isn't quite like that. We have to get used to picturing our relationship to the other, the spiritual world differently the moment we cross the threshold of the spiritual world. We have to accept in total earnestness what has repeatedly been said, namely that the moment we make even just one step into the spiritual world—meaning that we expand our powers of observation—we grow together, so to say, with the beings that are around us, we extend our own being over them. And I have used the trivial, not pretty but effective expression: we crawl into those beings, we grow together with them. On the physical plane we always feel that the beings are outside us, and that which we observe of them comes into us. In the case of beings of the higher worlds we have to feel that we enter into them. And just as the beings of the mineral, plant, and animal kingdoms let themselves be observed by us, so must we let ourselves be observed by the beings of the higher hierarchies; this means that we become objective objects of observation for the beings of the higher hierarchies. I would say: just as the various animals are spread out here in space, so that we can observe them, just so are we observed by the beings of the higher hierarchies. They look at us. And the fact that they look at us is something we experience; observation by the higher beings actually consists in this. One should therefore not say: I observe an Angel—because that does not exactly reflect the experience—but: I sense, I feel that I am being observed by an Angel.

Surrendering our thinking to the Angels, so that they think in us

Rudolf Steiner, *The Fifth Gospel* (CW 148), December 18, 1913:

You must know that you are not governing your own thoughts in your conscious mind, but that the spirits of the next hierarchy are governing them. You must feel the conscious awareness of the Angels welling and actively moving within you. This will give you insight into the progressive impulses of evolution, for instance, the truth about the Christ impulse, which continues to be active today, seeing that it has come into existence. The Angels are able to think those impulses; we human beings are able to think and characterize them if our attitude to our thoughts is one where we give them over to the Angels, letting them think in us. This is achieved by long training, as described in my book *How to Know Higher Worlds*. A moment comes when the words "Your soul no longer thinks; it is a thought which the Angels are thinking" become meaningful, something you can feel. When this becomes true individual human experience, you inwardly enter into the thoughts of the general Christ truths, let us say, or other thoughts concerning the wise guidance of Earth evolution.

For the Spirit's world-thoughts hold sway
in cosmic being, imploring light.

The color-breathing conversation of the Angeloi, Archangeloi, Archai

The Angeloi, Archangeloi, Archai breathe colors, world thoughts. They awaken these thoughts to life and turn to the Exousiai, Dynameis, Kyriotetes, who awaken these enlivened thoughts into existence. Out of this a new world will come into being.

Rudolf Steiner, *The First Class Lessons and Mantras,* seventeenth lesson:

My dear sisters and brothers, let us place this image before our souls once again. We see the cosmic chalice spanning half the sky with colors flooding it within. We normally see such colors interweaving and living in one another only on the surface of the rainbow, but here they approach us as beings from the third hierarchy: Angeloi, Archangeloi, and Archai. The thoughts of the beings of the third hierarchy become visible for our soul in this breathing of color.

We observe how the beings of the third hierarchy, permeated with these cosmic thoughts, turn to the beings of the second hierarchy whom they serve: the Exousiai, Dynameis, and Kyriotetes. This powerful image stands before us: pure spiritual beings appear, residents of the sun, who only appear when the physical image cast by the sun disappears. Despite the magnitude of the sun in comparison with the Earth, it is a small image, only an image. The infinitely larger sun majestically fills the entire universe when this great cosmic image disappears. Then the beings of the second hierarchy appear, weaving and living in the realm of pure spirit, receiving what the Angeloi, Archangeloi, and Archai bring them. These are not dead thoughts such as we have. Dead thoughts are taken from the mirage of the senses and become living thoughts through the breathing of the Angeloi, Archangeloi, and Archai. In a mighty offering the Angeloi, Archangeloi, and Archai place these living thoughts before the second hierarchy. Thoughts that were only illusions, only semblances in earthly life, are awakened into being by the second hierarchy.

We see how the beings of the second hierarchy receive the thoughts that have been brought to life by the third hierarchy. And now, like a mighty resurrection, a new world comes into being. The Angeloi, Archangeloi, and Archai receive and take up what was dead substance from the world of sense-illusion. Then through the activity of the Exousiai, Dynameis, and Kyriotetes a new world comes into being, a world arising from what was dead.

Archai – Archangeloi – Angeloi
Let from the depths be entreated
what in the heights is heard
then it speaks through the world
Per Spiritum Sanctum reviviscimus.

Where are the Angels?

They are just as countless and dynamic as thought powers

Rudolf Steiner, *The Spiritual Hierarchies and the Physical World* (CW 110), April 16, 1909:

When one meets human beings, it is obvious that they carry their members within them—everything is differentiated organically. But if you want to find an Angel, you must remember that an Angel's physical aspect here below is a reflection of the spiritual principles visible only in the supersensible world. You will find the physical bodies of Angels in flowing water, in mist rising from evaporating bodies of water, and in the wind and lightning flashing through the air, as well as other occurrences of this kind.

One of the first stumbling blocks for the human being is the firm conviction that a physical body must have a definite boundary. As human beings we find it difficult to say to ourselves: I stand in a rising or falling mist or before a spraying brook. I am surrounded by the rushing, roaring wind. I see lightning flashing in the clouds. These are the revelations of the Angels. I need to see that beyond this physical manifestation, which is not as narrowly defined as the human one, is a manifestation of a spiritual body.

As human beings we develop all of the members of our being as self-enclosed entities. That is why we cannot imagine that the physical body can appear hazy and indistinct, that it may float and hover in the air, that it need not have definitely outlined contours. You must imagine, for example, that eighty Angels may have the densest part of their physical nature in one stretch of water. We should not imagine that the physical body of an Angel needs to be limited in any way. An Angel can belong to a portion of water here; far away is another segment. In short, we see that everything that surrounds us as water, air, and fire on earth must be so conceived as to contain the bodies of beings belonging to the hierarchy immediately above humanity.

To behold the I and manas of angelic beings, however, we need clairvoyant sight in the astral world. Angelic beings look down upon us from higher worlds. To find them we must investigate the realm of the solar system that extends as far as the orbit of the moon.

[...]

You would have to look for the Archangel's spiritual counterpart, which is manifest in the rushing wind and fire, clairvoyantly in the spiritual world.

[...]

The physical bodies of the Archai can be perceived only in flames of fire.

Michael as a sun among the Archangels

Rudolf Steiner, *Approaching the Mystery of Golgotha* (CW 152), May 2, 1913:

The being we may call Michael, who belongs to the hierarchy of the Archangels—however we might wish to call this being—nonetheless exists. And there are many beings of this sort who belong to the same rank. However, this particular being, who is known esoterically as Michael, is as exalted among his companions as the Sun is with respect to the planets—Venus, Mercury, Jupiter, Saturn, etc. Michael is the most excellent and significant being in the hierarchy of the Archangels. The ancients called Michael "God's countenance."

The trinity of earth, planets, fixed stars and the trinity of thinking, feeling, will

"Let from the depths be entreated what in the heights will be heard." The German word erbitten *is usually translated as* to ask. *But in the most encompassing German digital dictionary DWDS you also find more subtle meanings and examples, such as* to beg, to entreat, *as in* Gottes Segen erbitten—implore God's blessing. *This meaning fits best here. And thus we find in the English version* to entreat, *the soul exercise as described in the Contemplation below. This indicates ascending to a truly religious experience of the world, and a mood that grows into a kind of prayer. Then we will feel ourselves as spirits in the spirit world, reborn in the spirit: "Per Spiritum Sanctum reviviscimus." If we then continue the exercise we will be allowed to experience the Trinity in the fixed stars, in the planets, and in the earth, but also inwardly in our thinking, feeling, and will. Thus, if it is given us, we may experience the Divine Trinity in everything within us and in everything around us.*

Rudolf Steiner, *The First Class Lessons and Mantras,* ninth lesson:

We realize and experience the spirit in us when we lift up our spirits to the fixed stars that shine down on us in their constellations, forms, and figures and thus become like a celestial script. If we preserve what is thus written in the starry heavens, then we shall become aware of our spirituality—a spirituality that does not address the human being personally, but speaks about the whole universe:

> *O Man, preserve in your spirit's creativity*
> *The heavenly revelation of the stars immobile.*

Summing this up:

> *O Man, create yourself through heaven's wisdom.*

Not through vague generalities, nor through vague sensations, will we be increasingly able to succeed in freeing our souls from our body and go out into the universe. We will be able to do all this, but only in the clear and specific way shown here, by grasping one element after another, by grasping the movement of the planets and the meaning of the stars. If we do this, we unite with the world.

[...]

But then, if this is really undergone and if by means of such an exercise we finally end up in a mood of piety, the world ceases to be physical for us. Then we say to ourselves with complete inner truth: the physical aspect of the world is only semblance; it is only Maya. Everywhere the world is spirit, through and through. As human beings we belong to the spirit. If we feel ourselves as a spirit in the spiritual world, we are on the other side of the threshold.

However, once we are on the other side of the threshold we sense how here on this side of the threshold our body holds thinking, feeling, and willing together through its own bodily force. We sense how the minute we are free from our body, our thinking, feeling, and willing are no longer one but are three. They are no longer unified but are threefold. Then, if we unite with the terrestrial forces of the earth, water, air, and fire, we send our will to the Earth and become one with the Earth through our will.

In addition, because we feel love in our soul for the movement of the planets (meaning we feel love for the spiritual beings who live there), we experience the powers orbiting in cosmic space as feeling. If we are able to say: the Sun moves in cosmic space as feeling; Mercury moves in cosmic space as feeling; Mars moves in cosmic space as feeling; then we have grasped feeling in its cosmic essence when it is separated from thinking and willing.

If we are able to take hold of thinking so that we can free our thoughts from physical existence, it is as though our thinking would fly far out to the stars and come to rest in the stars themselves. And when we have arrived at the other side of the threshold we can say to ourselves: my thinking is at rest in the stars; my feeling is moving with the planets; my willing unites with the forces of the Earth. Thinking, feeling, and willing are distributed in the universe in this manner.

They must be joined together again. Here on Earth we don't need to join thinking, feeling, and willing together because they are bound together as a unity due to our physical body. Thinking, feeling, and willing would continually fall apart if they were not held together by the physical human being without intending or willing it. But on the other side of the threshold they are separated. Thinking, feeling, and willing are separated so that thinking rests above with the stars; feeling is circling with the planets; and willing unites with the forces of the Earth below. Now we must—with strong, inner determination, by means of our own forces—bring these three back together again into a unity, the three that are far apart on the other side of the threshold.

To achieve this, which is possible through such mantras, we must experience thinking, feeling, and willing in such a way that we are able to communicate to thinking, which has gone out to the stars, something of feeling and willing; so that we are able to communicate to feeling, which is orbiting with the planets, something of thinking and willing; and, so that we can communicate to willing, which is bound to the Earth, something of feeling and thinking.

We must look up to the stars and say to ourselves with devotion: my thinking is at rest up there. But I will bring the starry sky into movement in the same way that feeling moves the planets. In spirit I will slowly move the starry sky; I feel attracted to the starry sky; I want to go up there and be one with the star-filled heavens. In this manner I incorporate feeling and willing into thinking, which is bound to the stars. Then I look up to the planets and feel: my own feeling wanders with these planets. But I will try to hold fast to the moment I beheld the ever-moving planets, holding it as fast as the stars are held fast in their positions. And with my entire "middle man," the central part of my nature, through all that belongs to heart and lungs, I will become one with the entire planetary system. Then I have imparted thinking and willing to feeling.

If through this mantric formula I now become aware of how, as a human being, I am bound to the Earth, I ought to add feeling and thinking to my earth-bound condition. I should bring the Earth into movement in thought so that I orbit the earth like a planet without perceiving its weight. Being earthbound becomes for me as if I carried the Earth along with me through cosmic space. Feeling is thereby mingled with will. Thinking is mixed with will when I move with the Earth in thought, but can also hold it still again, making the Earth into a fixed star through meditation and my own power of thought.

About the Rosicrucian sayings

Rudolf Steiner, *Esoteric Lessons* 1910–1912 (CW 266/2), August 26, 1910:

We have come into being through higher spiritual forces, as we have heard throughout these days. We have descended from the divine womb. We have a divine origin. Thus, out of this knowledge we can place before our souls the Rosicrucian saying: *Ex Deo nascimur*—out of God we are born. But another statement should stand right next to it, one that makes us feel much smaller, so that we surrender and lose ourselves; we devote ourselves to Christ. And when this mood properly lives in our soul, then we can add *In Christo morimur*, to *Ex Deo nascimur*. And as a further view of how we can consciously develop the spirit, the Holy Spirit within us, the Rosicrucian saying gives us the sentence that follows the first two sentences: *Per Spiritum Sanctum reviviscimus*—in the Holy Spirit we will live again and again.

The Meaning of Father, Son, and Spirit in the Rosicrucian sayings

Rudolf Steiner, *The Language of the Cosmos: Cosmic Influences and the Spiritual Task of Northern Europe* (CW 209), December 26, 1921:

Through the centuries, understanding of the resurrected one, the vanquisher of death, was lost more and more. Enlightened theology of more modern times has only recognized the human being Jesus of Nazareth. This human being Jesus of Nazareth cannot be the second beside the Father principle. He could proclaim the Father, but he could not, in the sense of the discussions of early Christianity, place himself beside the Father. But on a par with each other stand the divine Father, who brings about the transition from the supersensory to the sensory—*Ex Deo nascimur*—and the divine Son, who brings about the transition from the sensory to the supersensory—*In Christo morimur*. And elevated over both, over birth and death, is a third principle, which emanates from both and is related on a par with both the divine Father and the divine Son: the Spirit, the Holy Spirit. Thus in the human being we recognize the transition from the supersensory to the sensory—*Ex Deo nascimur*—the transition from the sensory to the supersensory—*In Christo morimur*—and the union of both, the union with that wherein neither birth nor death have reality any longer, the resurrection through the Spirit: *Per Spiritum Sanctum reviviscimus*.

This is heard by the spirits of the elements
in east, west, north, south
may human beings hear it.

Character sketch of the elemental beings

From a lecture given six weeks before the Foundation Stone Meditation (continuation of the character sketch given for the second panel)

Rudolf Steiner, *Harmony of the Creative Word: The Human Being and the Elemental, Animal, Plant and Mineral Kingdoms* (CW 230), November 4, 1923:

Now we are going from the gnomes to the undines, the water beings. That is actually a very remarkable picture. These beings do not have the urge to life that human beings have, neither the urge to life that the animals even instinctively have, but one could almost say: the undines, and also the sylphs, have an urge to die. In a cosmic way they are really like the moth that flies into a flame. They have the feeling that they really only have their life when they die. It is extraordinarily interesting: here on the physical earth everything wants to live, and one values actually everything that has life force in it; one values everything that sprouts and germinates. But when we come to the other side, all these beings tell us: dying, that is actually the right beginning of life. And these beings can really experience this.

Let's take these undines. You know perhaps that, for instance, mariners, who are often sailing on the seas, feel that the sea makes a very special impression, such as the Baltic Sea in July, August, September, and that these people say: the sea starts to blossom. In a way it sprouts, but it sprouts from all that is disintegrating in the sea. The disintegration of the sea happens there; it gives the sea a characteristic bad smell.

But all of this is different for the undines. It is not at all unpleasant for the undines. When these millions and millions of water animals disintegrate in the sea, the sea becomes something that shines up in the most wonderful phosphorescent play of colors. Everything shines and glitters in all possible colors. They see glittering especially in blueish, purplish, and greenish colors. The whole disintegration process in the sea thus becomes a glimmering, glistening in the darker colors and into green. But these colors are realities for the undines, and one can then see how they take these colors into themselves in this play of colors of the sea. They pull these colors into their own corporeality. They become the way these color plays are; they become phosphorescent themselves.

And as they take these color plays in and become phosphorescent themselves, a kind of longing arises in them, a great longing to go up, to float up. This longing makes them float upward, and they offer themselves to the beings of the higher hierarchies, the Angeloi, Archangeloi, etc., as earthly nourishment. They find their fulfillment in this. They thus live further amid the higher hierarchies.

It is remarkable how these beings develop, one may say, in every early spring out of unfathomable depths. They are part of the life of the earth by working in the plant kingdom in the way I have described. Then, in a certain sense, they pour themselves into water, absorb through their own corporeality the phosphorescent water, that which is disintegrating, and in great longing bear it up. One can see in a colossal, grandiose world image how the colors born by the undines arise from the earth water, the colors that are spiritual-substantive, how they offer the beings of the higher hierarchies their nourishment, how the earth becomes a source of nourishment for the higher hierarchies because the longing of the undines consists in letting themselves be consumed by higher beings. Thus they live on; thus in a certain sense they enter eternity.

Now we are going to the sylphs. In the course of the year we come across dying birds. I have sketched for you how dying birds have their spiritual substance, and how they want to give this spiritual over to higher worlds, so that it rises up from the earth. But this asks for mediators. These mediators are the sylphs. For indeed, through the dying bird world astrality is constantly added to the air, admittedly a lower astrality, but still it contains astral substance. In this astral substance, I cannot say flutter, I would say float the sylphs. They absorb what comes out of the dying bird world, bear it longingly up into the heights again, and want to be breathed in by the beings of the higher hierarchies. They offer themselves as a breath element to the higher hierarchies.

Again a grandiose spectacle! As one sees the bird world dying this astral, inwardly shining substance goes into the air. The sylphs flicker like blue lightning through the air, and in their blue flickers, first greenish then becoming more red, they take this astrality that comes from the bird world and whisk it away like upward flashing lighting. If we follow this beyond space, then they become breathed in by the beings of the higher hierarchies, so that one may say: the gnomes change one world into another in its structure; in a certain sense they accompany evolution horizontally. The other beings, the undines and sylphs, bear upward what they feel in their own dying, in being enjoyed, in being breathed in. They then live on in the higher hierarchies, in which they find their eternity.

And when one then goes on to the fire beings—yes, my dear friends, just imagine how butterfly dust from butterfly wings seemingly disappears into nothingness as the butterfly dies. But it isn't true that it disappears into nothingness. That which blows away from butterfly wings is highly spiritualized matter. All of it flows into the warmth ether that surrounds the earth like tiny little comets, each individual grain of dust like a tiny comet in the warmth ether. When the butterfly world comes to an end in the course of the year, everything becomes glittering and shining. And it glimmers and shines in them, and they also become filled with longing. They bear that which they have so absorbed into the heights.

And one can see—I have described it for you from another side—how that which is born up from the butterfly wings by the fire beings, glitters in the world-all. But it not only glitters, it streams out, and this is what gives the spirits of the higher hierarchies their view of the earth. The spirits of the higher hierarchies look upon the earth and see especially this essence of butterfly and insect being that is carried upward by the fire beings. And the fire beings find their highest satisfaction in sensing that they are the ones that become visible to the spiritual vision of the higher hierarchies. They find their greatest bliss in being observed by the higher hierarchies. They strive toward these higher hierarchies and bring them knowledge of the earth.

So you see how these elemental beings are mediators between the earth and the spiritual cosmos: this spectacle of the upward rising phosphorescent undines that disappear into the light and fire sea of the higher hierarchies as nourishment, the upward jerking greenish-reddish flashes of the sylphs that are breathed where the earthly continually changes into the eternal, and the eternal existence of the fire beings, whose work is lasting. For while here on earth the birds die only in a specific season, these fire beings see to it that what is visible of them streams into the world-all throughout the year. Thus the earth wears a kind of fire mantle around it. From the outside it looks fiery.

But the whole is brought about by beings who see the things of the earth very differently from the human being. As was said before, human beings experience the earth as hard substance, on which they can stand and go about. For the gnomes it is a transparent globe, a hollow globe. For the undines water is something in which they observe, absorb, and experience phosphorescence. For the sylphs the astrality of the air, which comes from dying birds, makes them become flashing lightning even more than they were already; otherwise they are like faint, blueish lightning. And the passing away of butterfly beings is something that, so to say, surrounds the earth as if it is enveloped by fire.

The earth looks as if the earth is in a certain way surrounded by a wonderful fiery picture, and on the one side, when one looks up from the earth, are those flickering flashes, those phosphorescent and disappearing undines. All this is as if we would have to say: Here on earth live and weave these elemental beings; they strive upward and disappear into the fire mantle of the earth. But they do not really disappear but find their eternal being there as they become one with the beings of the higher hierarchies.

Everything we see there like a wonderful world picture is an expression of what takes place on the earth; in its beginning stage it happens on the earth. We human beings are part of what takes place there, and even when human beings are not able to understand this with their usual consciousness, we are part of the activities of these beings every night; in our I and astral body we take part in what these beings are doing.

Especially for the gnomes it is amusing to observe human beings when they are asleep, not the physical body in the bed, but the human beings who are outside the physical body as an I and astral body, and to see that human beings actually think in the spirit and don't know it. They do not know that their thoughts live in the spirit. And again, for the undines it is inexplicable that human beings know themselves so little; and it is the same for the sylphs and the fire beings. You see, physically it is an unpleasant idea to have mosquitos and such flitting around you. But in the case of the spiritual human being, the I and the astral body, these elemental beings weave and live around them at night, and this actually gives us a continual impetus to develop our consciousness further, so that we learn to know more about the world.

Contemplations for the Fourth Panel

At the turning point of time
the spirit-light of the world
entered the stream of earth existence.

The cosmic dimension of the crucifixion and resurrection of Christ

Rudolf Steiner, *Die menschliche Seele in ihrem Zusammenhang mit göttlich-geistigen Individualitäten* [The human soul in relation to divine-spiritual individualities] (CW 224), April 13, 1923:

Before the Mystery of Golgotha the actual event of death in life was not an experience of the gods. Death came into life due to luciferic and ahrimanic influences—by divine beings that were staying behind or storming ahead too fast. But death was actually not something that was an experience of the higher hierarchies. It did not become an experience of the higher hierarchies until the moment when the Christ went through the Mystery of Golgotha, in other words, went through death; when Christ united Himself with the destiny of humanity so deeply that He wanted to have in common with earthly humanity that He went through death. The event of Golgotha is therefore not merely an event of earthly life, it is an event of divine life. What took place on the earth, and what grew in the human soul as insight in the event of Golgotha, these are reflections of something that is far more encompassing, magnificent, tremendous, sublime that took place in the world of the gods itself. And Christ's passage through death on Golgotha is an event through which the first hierarchy reached up into a higher realm.

Darkness of night
had ceased its reign.

The power of darkness

Rudolf Steiner, *The Fifth Gospel* (CW 148), December 18, 1913:

This led to the great council of the gods arriving at something like the following conclusion: "As we have not been able to keep Lucifer and Ahriman away from Earth evolution, our servants, the Angels, Archangels, and Archai, are no longer able, from a certain point in time, to do what we intend them to do for humanity." The point in time was that of the Mystery of Golgotha.

When this time approached the gods of the highest hierarchies had to say to themselves: "We are losing the possibility of letting our servants intervene in human souls. We have been unable to hold off Lucifer and Ahriman and because of this we shall not be able to influence evolution through our servants after this time. Then powers will arise in human souls that can no longer be guided by Angels, Archangels, and Archai. Human beings are getting beyond our reach because of the powers of Lucifer and Ahriman."

That truly was the "mood" in heaven when the moment in time approached that marked the beginning of our present era. The gods' great "anxiety" was that their servants would no longer be able to look after humanity properly from a certain point in time. I am sure you will not misunderstand this, for you know from the science of the spirit that terms have a different meaning and evoke a different response when we use them to characterize the higher worlds.

The gods' "anxiety" grew, becoming more and more of a torment, if we may put it like this. Then the decision was made to send down the Sun spirit, sacrificing it, for they said to themselves: "Let him choose a different destiny from now on. Instead of sitting in the council of the gods let him enter the arena where human souls live. We sacrifice this Sun spirit who until now has been one of us in the spheres of the higher hierarchies. Now he shall enter into the Earth's aura, and Jesus shall be the gateway for this."

Day-radiant light
shone forth in human souls
light
that gives warmth
to simple shepherds' hearts
light
that enlightens
the wise heads of kings.

Christ brought all the abundance of the streaming sun power to the earth

Rudolf Steiner, *According to Matthew* (CW 123), September 10, 1910:

Egohood was once present in a personality on the earth in such full measure that if human beings receive Christ into themselves in the sense indicated by St. Paul, they will themselves acquire in the course of successive incarnations the forces and power of this Egohood. As they pass from incarnation to incarnation during the rest of earthly evolution, human beings who imbue their souls with the power of that personality who once lived on the earth, will rise to greater and greater heights. At that time, chosen ones were able with their physical eyes to behold Christ in the body of Jesus of Nazareth. Once in the course of the earth's evolution, and for the sake of mankind, Christ, who formerly could only be revealed to human vision as the Spirit of the Sun, descended and united Himself with the forces of the earth.

It is the human being in whom the power of the sun was to be present in its fullness—the power of the sun that was once to descend and work in a human physical body. This was the inauguration of the epoch during which the forces outpoured from the sun will flow in ever greater measure into humanity as people live on from incarnation to incarnation, and—as far as the earthly body permits—gradually permeate themselves with the Christ power.

What was the message the Angels proclaimed to the shepherds?

Rudolf Steiner, *According to Luke* (CW 114), September 16, 1909:

A wonderful passage in the Gospel of St. Luke describes how an Angel appeared to the shepherds in the fields and announced to them that the Savior of the world was born. Then come the words: "And suddenly there was with the Angel a multitude of the heavenly host." Picture the scene to yourselves: as the shepherds look upward the heavens open and the beings of the spiritual world are revealed in sublime pictures.

What was the proclamation to the shepherds? It was clothed in momentous words, words that resounded through the whole of evolution and have become the Christmas message. Rightly rendered, these words would be as follows: "The Divine Beings manifest themselves from on high, that peace may reign on the earth below among human beings who are filled with good will!" The usual expression "glory" is entirely out of place here. The sentence is correct in the form I have now given, and the contrast should be clearly emphasized. What the shepherds saw was the manifestation of spiritual beings from on high, and the revelation occurred when it did in order that peace might pour into human hearts that were filled with a good will. As we shall see, many mysteries of Christianity are embodied in these words, provided only they are rightly understood.

The Gospel originates in the sphere of the Angels and Archangels

Rudolf Steiner, *The Gospel of St. Mark* (CW 139), September 15, 1912:

What then is the Gospel? It is something that comes down to us from the kingdoms we have often described, where dwell the higher hierarchical beings, among whom are the Angels and Archangels. It descends through the world that rises above the human world. Thus we gain an inkling of the deeper meaning of the word Gospel. It is an impulse that descends through the realm of the Archangels and Angels; it comes down from these kingdoms and enters into mankind.

None of the abstract translations really cover the matter adequately. In reality the word Gospel should indicate that at a certain time something begins to flow in upon the earth which formerly flowed only where there dwell the Angels and Archangels. Something descended to earth that shook the souls of human beings and shook the strongest souls most. It is here noted that this was the beginning, and the beginning has a continuation. The beginning was made at that time, and we shall see that fundamentally the whole development of humanity since then is a continuation of that beginning when the impulse began to flow down from the kingdom of the Angeloi, or what we call the "ev-angel" or Gospel.

Light divine

Christ-Sun

warm our hearts

enlighten our heads

The outer appearance of the higher hierarchies

Toward the end, the Foundation Stone Meditation begins to take on the character of a kind of prayer. All the beings of the hierarchies are carried by love, by profound inner love, which outwardly appears as light!

Rudolf Steiner, *The Book of Revelation and the Work of the Priest* (CW 346), September 19, 1924:

The world-all consists in its inner substance and essence, to the extent that it is the universe of the human being, of pure love; it is nothing but pure love. Within the Divine that is associated with humanity we find nothing but pure love. But this love is really an inner love, it can be inwardly experienced in the soul. It would never come to outer manifestation if it did not first built its body out of the element, the etheric element of light. And when we rightly observe the occult world it will be natural for us to say to ourselves: the primary essence of the world is the inner essence of love, outwardly appearing as light. This is not a conviction based on faith of a person who has insight into these things, but it is fully objectively gained knowledge. The world-all, in which the human being is rooted, is inwardly essential love, outwardly appearing as light. Essential—this applies to all the beings of the higher hierarchies, who are borne by this love and inwardly experience this love. However, if we want to use an abstract idea, it appears as light. The outer appearance of these beings is love; the outer appearance of love is light.

That good may become
what from our hearts
we are founding
what from our heads
we direct
with focused will.

Angelic beings in our thinking, feeling, and will

This collection of contemplations opened with the path of reverence, as the beginning of the path of schooling. When Rudolf Steiner laid the Foundation Stone Meditation in the hearts of the members, the final words became, as path of reverence, the leading principle underlying the foundation and purposeful leadership of the worldwide Anthroposophical Society. And now, in our time, these words may inspire and guide us in taking new initiatives, and also as we jointly carry the work within the anthroposophical movement and beyond.

We may in this connection call to mind the words Rudolf Steiner spoke as "a kind of prayer" during the preparations for the first Waldorf School in 1919. These are words from which many teachers' colleges worldwide have received and continue to receive inspiration. The official publication of these words with permission of the leaders of the School of Spiritual Science has also enabled other working groups to be inspired by them. These words are about mutual understanding, about cooperation, about responsibility, and about the role of the Angels and Archangels in this process. All those who want to take an initiative in true co-responsibility, or want to carry out an initiative, may take these words to heart.

Rudolf Steiner did not allow this prayer to be recorded. Two of those present wrote the text down from memory, Caroline von Heydebrand and Herbert Hahn. Below follows the rendition by the latter.

Rudolf Steiner, *The Foundations of Human Experience* (CW 293), notes made by Herbert Hahn from memory after Steiner's lecture of August 21, 1919 to the future teachers of the Waldorf School in Stuttgart:

In that we actively turn to the pedagogy of this fifth cultural epoch, and in that we wish to be active as teachers, we may carry in consciousness the fact that the beings of the third hierarchy are now moving to connect themselves with our work.

Behind each individual member of the now-forming faculty, we see an Angel standing. He lays both hands upon the head of the earthly being entrusted to him, and in this position and with this gesture allows *strength* to flow over to the human. It is the strength that provides the Imaginations necessary for the deed to be completed. Creatively imagining, awakening powerful Imaginations, the Angel thus stands behind each individual.

Raising our view higher, we see hovering above the heads of this forming faculty a host of Archangels. Circling again and again, they carry from each of us to the other what results from our spiritual encounter with our own Angel. And they carry it, enriched by the strength of all the others, back to us. In this circle, which acts like an activity of spiritual formation, a vessel is formed above the heads of those united in this common striving. This vessel is formed from a specific substance—courage. At the same time, these circling, connecting Archangels allow creatively inspirational forces to enter into their movements. The Archangels open the source for those inspirations necessary for our work.

Raising our view still higher, it rises to the realm of the Archai. They are not represented in their entirety. However, from their realm, the realm of light, they let a drop descend into the vessel of courage. We feel that this drop of light is given to us from the good Spirit of our Time, who stands behind the founder and the founding of this new school. It is the creative forces of intuition at work in this drop of light. The Archai want to awaken the necessary intuition in those now entering this new pedagogical work.

Giving strength, courage, and light, beings of the third hierarchy take part in what is now being founded. Imaginatively, inspiringly, intuitively, they wish to connect with our earthly deeds.

Notes and Concluding Comments

TEXT AND TRANSLATION

The version of the Foundation Stone Meditation used in this book is partly based on the modernized English translation of the version Rudolf Steiner published in print in the *Nachrichtenblatt* of January 13, 1924. I adapted the text, however, at some points to the words he spoke in the days of the Christmas Conference from Christmas Day 1923 to New Years's Day 1924, morning and evening, in nine slightly differing oral versions, in which the Foundation Stone Meditation was "laid and sunk into our hearts," as he called it. One reason for these adaptations is to approach Rudolf Steiner's choice of words as closely as possible, and to accentuate the freshness and speed of his words.

The other reason is the inner meaning of the angelic hierarchies and their names Rudolf Steiner evoked. These names are an important aid toward insight into the structure and the mutual relationships between these nine groups of angels. Ever since the fall of the year 1900, Rudolf Steiner characterized them time and again, using a rich variety of names, as he built anthroposophy in its fullness on the clear threefold structure of the angelic hierarchies. In the *Nachrichtenblatt* he summarized their Hebrew and Greek names as *Spirits of Strength, Spirits of Light, and Spirits of Soul,* which perfectly characterizes these three angelic hierarchies. However, their nine names provide, on the one hand, a more direct and clearer connection to the basic structure of anthroposophy as Rudolf Steiner had previously described it in *An Outline of Esoteric Science.* On the other hand, the evocation of these nine names can be felt as a prelude to his grand series of *Esoteric Lessons*, which he would start six weeks after the Christmas Conference.

In the printed version in the *Nachrichtenblatt* there are more deviations from the previously spoken words. For example, in the printed version the three Rosicrucian sayings were each introduced by the words *Dies spricht* (translated as *Speaking*). Orally however, during the eight day of the Conference, Rudolf Steiner introduced these Rosicrucian words in a number of different ways: *Dieses spricht – das spricht – und es spricht – es spricht – dann spricht es durch die Welt* (*This speaks – that speaks – and it speaks – it speaks – then it speaks throughout the world).* The last six words were connected to those before them in the same sentence: *O let from the depths be entreated what in the heights can be heard*—instead of *will be heard*, as the printed version has it. As long as we only entreat or pray what *can* be heard in the heights, it will evoke the sphere of Pentecost and it will speak through the world.

May these oral variations on the usual printed version inspire the reader to new thoughts and new feelings about this wonderful gemstone, which is the Foundation Stone Meditation.

You will find still more variations in the texts of December 25, 26, 27, 28, 29, 30, 31, 1923 and the two texts of January 1, 1924, morning and evening, in the book *The Christmas Conference for the Foundation of the General Anthroposophical Society 1923–1924*, CW 260, by Rudolf Steiner.

The Hierarchies

Rudolf Steiner frequently used the term *höhere Geister—higher Spirits.* This might lead us to think of "higher ones" between the hierarchies of angels, but that proves to be an error. The term refers to all hierarchies higher than our human, fourth hierarchy.

Also, the term *angels* is, on the one hand, a general one for all the hierarchies but, on the other hand, it is also the name of the hierarchy closest to the human being, which can light up in our thinking power because those Angels are themselves thinking powers. When referring to the latter I have capitalized the word Angel. The distinction between the two meanings of the term *angeloi* (angels) is as old as ancient esoteric Christianity.

Rudolf Steiner sometimes referred to the first and second hierarchies as "gods" (*Götter*), and the second and third hierarchy he sometimes also called "spirits" (*Geister*). He used these terms quite freely, and with many exceptions. The terms were actually used interchangeably. This is also the case with the numbering of the hierarchies. Usually, the highest hierarchy is called the "first," and the lowest the "third." But sometimes Rudolf Steiner reversed this. Then he called the lowest one the "first" (closest to humanity) and the highest the "third" (the most remote). The reason for this is unknown to me, but the effect is that we must be fully awake as we are reading.

The hierarchies of the angels were time and again invoked by Rudolf Steiner by their Hebrew and Greek names. For this reason, those names are capitalized in this book, even though because of their often plural form they may also be understood as generic names.

FROM RUDOLF STEINER'S LIFE

UNTIL THE YEAR 1900 Rudolf Steiner was mostly known as a co-worker in the Goethe Archives and as a philosopher who actively participated in the philosophical discussions of his time. He was a well-known orator. For example, at the 500-year memorial of the art of printing in the summer of 1900 he made the festive speech before 7000 assembled printers and typesetters. In October 1900 he began in the Theosophical Library in Berlin with a big series of lectures about mysticism which later became the book *Mysticism at the Dawn of the Modern Age*.

In that lecture cycle he brought purely Christian, western spirituality to a public consisting of theosophists who were oriented toward oriental wisdom. The entire cycle was about Christian mystics, especially Master Eckhardt and John Scotus Eriugena, who strongly built on early esoteric Christianity, particularly on the writings of Dionysius the Areopagite.

Later he explained that this Dionysius "systematized" the hierarchies of the angels, and that the essence of his teaching is exactly the same as anthroposophy. Steiner built his anthroposophy on the foundation of this doctrine of the hierarchies, with an impressive crescendo in the last year of his life. See also the Introduction of this book.

ABOUT THE AUTHOR

MICHIEL TER HORST (1941) made a commitment to anthroposophy as the founder and board member of *Akwarius*, a wholesaler in biodynamic agricultural products, of *De Oorsprong* (*The Origin*), an organic store, the Waldorf School in Alphen on the Rhine, and of the *Stichting Rudolf Steiner Vertalingen* (*Foundation Rudolf Steiner Translations*). He was a mentor at the *Vrije Hogeschool* (*Waldorf College*) from 1978, then became its Chairman in 1997. And from 1974 to 2013 he was at first Treasurer, later President of the *Iona Stichting* (*Iona Foundation*). He translated the most important Greek text from early esoteric Christianity into Dutch: *Dionysius the Areopagite, Verzamelde Werken* (*Collected Works*), published by Uitgeverij Christofoor 2015.

ENDNOTES

1. Rudolf Steiner, *The Fifth Gospel* (CW 148), December 18, 1913.
2. Dionysius the Areopagite, *About the Heavenly Hierarchy*, no. 332 A–D.
3. Rudolf Steiner, *The Fourth Dimension* (CW 324a), Question and Answer Session, April 21, 1909.
4. Rudolf Steiner, *Genesis* (CW 122), August 22, 1910, Rosicrucian sayings.
5. Rudolf Steiner, *The Spiritual Hierarchies and Their Reflection in the Physical World* (CW 110), Düsseldorf 1909.
6. Rudolf Steiner, *The Principle of Spiritual Economy* (CW 109), March 31, 1909.
7. Rudolf Steiner, *The Language of the Cosmos*, (CW 209), December 26, 1921.
8. All quotations of First Class texts are taken from: T. H. Meyer (ed.), *The First Class Lessons and Mantras* (SteinerBooks, 2017).
9. Rudolf Steiner, *Theosophy* (CW 9), Anthroposophic Press, 1994.
10. Rudolf Steiner, *Mystics at the Dawn of the Modern Age* (CW 7).